Randy Nelson

Poachers, Polluters & Politics

POACHERS, POLLUTERS
& Politics

A Fishery Officer's Career

RANDY NELSON

HARBOUR PUBLISHING

1 2 3 4 5 —18 17 16 15 14

Harbour Publishing Co. Ltd.
P.O. Box 219, Madeira Park, BC, V0N 2H0
www.harbourpublishing.com

Cover illustration by Kim La Fave
Interior photographs from the author's collection
Edited by Ian Whitelaw
Cover design by Anna Comfort O'Keeffe and Carleton Wilson
Text design by Mary White
Printed and bound in Canada

Harbour Publishing acknowledges financial support from the Government of Canada through the Canada Book Fund and the Canada Council for the Arts, and from the Province of British Columbia through the BC Arts Council and the Book Publishing Tax Credit.

Cataloguing data available from Library and Archives Canada
ISBN 978-1-55017-639-1 (paperback)
ISBN 978-1-55017-641-4 (ebook)

This book is dedicated to fallen fish and wildlife officers in North America; those who have lost their lives conserving and protecting our renewable resources. This book is also for my late father, Carl, a Saskatchewan farmer and pioneer, a man who loved to read despite having to leave school in Grade 8 to help care for his younger siblings following their mother's death. He helped me realize intelligence has little to do with education.

I'd also like to thank those that gave permission to include their names with the understanding that this book may not reflect their personal views and opinions.

Contents

Introduction

A seasonal officer and I took a canoe down the Lakelse River near Terrace, BC, to count spawning salmon one fall day. Raised on a farm in Saskatchewan, I had had little experience on the water, but the officer had several years of canoeing background.

Spawning salmon were everywhere. We paddled past a couple of black bears and were generally having a fantastic day in the field. We rounded a curve in the river and saw a sizeable logjam ahead. We'd have to stop and carry our canoe over a small section. We pulled our canoe parallel to a large three-foot-diameter cedar log and what happened next was so fast it was frightening.

The current caught our canoe just as Reg stepped up onto the large log. I grabbed the large, slippery cedar log and embedded my fingernails in it. The canoe was flipping over and my long legs and size thirteen feet were stuck under the seat of the canoe. The boat then turned completely upside down, contorting and twisting my body. My fingernails were starting to slip when the mahogany seat broke and the canoe disappeared under the logjam. I quickly pulled myself up onto the logs.

Reg and I stood in amazement as the canoe banged and bounced under the logjam. In about ten minutes it emerged downstream and we were able to catch up to it in some slack water and paddle to our truck. If things had gone just a little bit differently, this would have been a very short book (and someone else would have had to write it).

For fishery officers, there are occupational hazards even more terrifying than fast-flowing water and slippery logs. I've had to deal with more than the occasional angry axe-wielding, rock-throwing or shotgun-blasting fisherman.

And yet, there's nothing more rewarding than the satisfaction of chasing down bad guys and I found myself with a burning desire to document what has been an exciting, eventful, dangerous, scary and sometimes hilarious career as a fishery officer for the Department of Fisheries and Oceans (DFO). That said, where do you start writing a book? Despite this ambition, I don't read much, so my mind wandered back to high school in Saskatchewan over three decades earlier and the dreaded book reports that had to be written. Maybe I should have actually read some of those books. I would read the first and last paragraphs of a book, then the back cover, and I'd write my report. I did okay with that strategy, usually scoring a B, but my desire to read never really took off. There was a time in my late teens when pictorial magazines became an interest but, although others claim they did, I didn't read the articles.

The encouragement to write my stories down finally came from Bob Chartier, a retired civil servant who's authored several books. I told him a few tales about my career and he just told me to start writing. Over the years I became aware that others were interested in the stories when I told them to friends and co-workers.

I hope you enjoy them!

My First Business Attempt

I grew up near Hodgeville, Saskatchewan, the Coyote Capital of Canada as a sign on the edge of town proudly proclaims. As farm kids we didn't have much money, so I came up with a great business idea in Grade 9. I found a mail-order supplier of firecrackers in a town about eighty miles away (ironically, the business was a drugstore where my future mother-in-law was working) and I would order the firecrackers and sell them at school, doubling my investment. Things were going great until someone lit a firecracker at school right by little Jimmy's ear. Jimmy went home with ringing ears, followed by his parents calling the principal. The next day I was called into the principal's office for the first time in my life. I wasn't even aware what it was about until he asked me about the firecrackers. I told the truth and admitted I was the pusher. Later that day he approached me and told me I was expelled from school for three days. "I'm going to die! My parents will kill me!"

The principal didn't phone my parents, however, and presumably Jimmy's parents and I were the only ones who knew my sentence. I thought about telling my parents—but I thought more about not telling them. I tossed and turned all night, sweating

Here I am as a mischievous first-grader in Saskatchewan—not yet dreaming that I'd someday grow into a relentless poacher catcher.

and worrying. I often work well under pressure and this was one of those times. I had an idea! I'd pretend I was sick for three days and no one would know. I bet you're laughing at that idea, but read on. In the morning I stayed in bed until my mother came in and I told her I was feeling real sick (which wasn't entirely untrue). She told me I should stay home for the day. Wow, it worked! Then an hour later she came in to check on me. She felt my forehead. "Gee, you don't have a fever." I started to sweat as she left the room. How could I get a fever? Quick thinking brought another bright idea. I put a pillow over my face and blew into the pillow repeatedly. I could feel my face getting warmer. This should work. I kept going until I couldn't get any warmer and then I called her. She came in and felt my very warm forehead. Now she started feeling sympathetic, bringing me soup and drinks for the rest of the morning. I kept my face warm by continually blowing into the pillow. I survived day one.

By the next day I was getting very bored, but my boredom quickly abated when I thought what would happen if I got healthy. The three days eventually passed and no one ever found out about my expulsion. I never told anyone until twenty years later. My parents had taught me to always tell the truth—in this case it just took a bit longer. Perhaps it was this failed business venture that turned me to the public sector. I can't help but think that if my firecracker business hadn't failed I might have followed in the footsteps of another great business mind like Jim Pattison. We'll never know.

It All Started in Saskatchewan

I developed a love for the outdoors, being raised on a farm in southern Saskatchewan. Like many farming kids I spent many hours shooting gophers, picking rocks, shovelling manure and driving tractors. School came easy to me, and my parents wanted me to use my brain to become a veterinarian. I wanted to be a carpenter or an archeologist until I heard of a course in Saskatoon called Renewable Resources Technology. I applied and waited, but I soon found out everyone wanted to do that course and the college rarely chose kids right out of high school, so I began looking at university and archeology courses. I had just finished the paperwork to apply when I was notified I'd been accepted to the Renewable Resources course at Kelsey Institute of Applied Arts and Sciences in Saskatoon. My high school principal had phoned the college and said they should take me. I don't think he told them about the firecrackers.

I loaded up my blue 1968 GMC pickup and drove the three hours to Saskatoon, where I room and boarded for the first year. I shared a very small room with another student, and the landlady provided us with lunch each day that almost always consisted of peanut butter and dill pickle sandwiches. That's right! Virtually

Southern Saskatchewan, 1973 — Before getting a job as a conservation officer trainee, my summer jobs included shovelling grain with my father.

every day was peanut butter and dill pickle sandwiches! I survived the very intense first year in good shape and received a scholarship for my marks.

In 1975, summer jobs were everywhere and I chose to work for the Department of Northern Saskatchewan as a resource student (conservation officer trainee). I was sent to the scenic northern community of La Ronge and I worked a few weeks around La Ronge until someone heard I liked doing manual labour. Then I was sent to Missinipe, beside Otter Lake, about an hour north, and as I headed out the door my boss said, "By the way, there are a lot of fishing camps up there and there's a float-plane base. If you want you can check some of the fishermen as they return from the camps. Here's an appearance notice book — and good luck."

That was it for training. Eighteen years old and given the power to really spoil someone's fishing trip. I joined forces with an old man who cleaned up the campgrounds and cut and split firewood. I loved it, except the part where the old guy showed me how to clean a campground toilet. He used a scrub brush to remove most of the "residue" but demonstrated that for the really tough chunks you had to scrape them off with a fingernail. I thought, "Is that why you have such long fingernails and is that why they are so dirty?" I almost got sick when I remembered him peeling potatoes the night before, and I suddenly developed the urge to do all the cooking, even though I didn't have a clue where to start. I really did enjoy the work though. We'd just finished supper on the third day when I heard a float-plane engine. I decided to walk down to the dock and see what I could find.

My First Bust

I must have been quite a sight from the plane. I was eighteen years old with hair far too long for enforcement and I wore blue jeans with my patrol shirt because they didn't have uniform pants for me. I stood back and watched as the pilot helped four fishermen unload the plane. Several large, apparently heavy, coolers caught my attention. I approached the group, who seemed rather jovial until I identified myself as a conservation officer and opened the coolers. My brain said "Ca-ching!" and my mouth said, "Wow, you guys have a lot of fish!" They were rather quiet as I counted sixty-nine walleye over their limit. Little did they know that I was probably more nervous than they were. I thought back to our law enforcement class in Saskatoon. "Oh yes, I got an A in that. I'm okay," I thought as I started to gather their personal information and fishing licences.

They helped me carry the coolers up the hill to the shack I was staying in and I thanked them for being so helpful. I understood why they were so helpful once I found out they were all from Regina. People from Saskatchewan will usually help anyone. Three of the men were okay with the events and accepted their deserved fate. The fourth, however, wanted to talk to me in his cabin.

I put the fish and fishing gear away and then went to meet him. He had a beer on the table. He opened a second and handed it to me. I really liked beer, I was eighteen (therefore legal in Saskatchewan) and it was free. What a dilemma, but I said no as he disappointedly guzzled his beer and tried to convince me to let them go. He was a very smooth, quick talker but then he hit me with a surprise. He was an

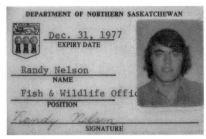

DEPARTMENT OF NORTHERN SASKATCHEWAN

Dec. 31, 1977
EXPIRY DATE

Randy Nelson
NAME

Fish & Wildlife Offic
POSITION

SIGNATURE

This long-haired teenager with a badge in Northern Saskatchewan sent many fishermen home with an empty cooler and a lighter wallet.

undercover RCMP officer and he claimed to be concerned about losing his job. I think he almost shed a tear. I'd always looked up to the Red Serge with unwavering admiration but it turns out some of them do bad things too. My instincts took over and I knew it would be totally wrong to ignore such a large violation. I let him babble on for about an hour before I left, saying he could discuss the matter with the Justice of the Peace (JP) the next day.

I made a late phone call to my boss to explain the situation and he gave me the name of the JP in Missinipe and discussed the paperwork I had to prepare for the next morning. I iced down the fish and spent until midnight typing the forms I needed for the appearance before the JP the next morning. A manual typewriter and carbon paper to make three copies were the tools. The forms had to be completed without any errors, without whiteout and without spell-check. I wasn't very confident the next day when I walked into the JP's office but my apprehension disappeared in a hurry as he complimented me on the job I'd done. An hour later the four men and I sat down in a small room to present the facts. I went first and told my story. Then the others all told their story, claiming three of them had caught the extra fish and the RCMP officer had stayed within his limit. I knew that was wrong but I hadn't taken a warned statement from any of them so I had to let them carry on. It was a lesson learned.

It's a sad reality but I learned to approach any violator with the thought they could be lying until proven otherwise. The three men received a hefty fine for those days ($200 each) plus forfeiture of their fishing gear and fish. They left rather unhappy and I left a whole lot wiser, or as wise as a long-haired eighteen-year-old with a badge could get. I resisted the urge to ask the RCMP officer if the free beer was still an option. Now my attention turned to the sixty-nine iced-down walleye. I didn't have freezer facilities so I called my boss, who told me to drive to La Ronge and take them to the commercial fishing plant to sell on behalf of the Crown. I headed down the road to deliver my first catch to the plant and then drove back to Missinipe. I was in a hurry because I didn't want to miss cooking my supper. I made it back in time.

Hey Boy! We Could Have You Fired!

After supper I heard another float plane coming in. I rushed down to the dock to meet three wealthy Americans with two large metal washtubs full of lake trout fillets. Wow! These guys were not happy and were certainly not used to being told what to do. They also couldn't count. "Hey boy! We could have you fired!" This was more difficult than the night before. They tried to take their fishing rods when I was counting the fish and I had to order them away from the dock until I was done. "We're never coming back here again," one barked. Oh, that was hard not to respond to. I told them to go to their cabin until I was done. (I couldn't help smiling inside; here I was at eighteen telling three adults to go to their room!) I packed the hundred-plus lake trout and the Americans' very expensive gear up to my cabin before heading over to see them.

It was a bit unnerving walking into their cabin. The three of them glared at me through their very expensive glasses of whisky and I thought, "If they offer me a free drink, this will be easy because I can't even stand the smell of Scotch." I took them outside one at a time to hear their stories and write the details down. Taking a warned statement became a habit I would keep forever and it saved me many, many times. Each of them admitted to catching about the same amount of fish. They were all concerned about their expensive fishing rods, telling me what they cost and how hard they were to get. I said I'd present the facts to the JP and they could tell him their side of the events. I arranged the hearing for the next morning, because they had to leave for the US, and spent another late night preparing paperwork. I iced the fish down and got some sleep.

I felt more confident and prepared the next day as I told the story to the JP. All three admitted to the facts but one really tried to get his rod back. He claimed it was a gift from his father and it really meant a lot to him. The JP asked me what I knew about this, so I took out my notebook and read the statement from the day before. The fisherman who'd claimed he'd received it as a gift had actually told me it cost him over $300. The JP gave the man an extra $100 fine and he forfeited his rod along with all the fish.

Little did I know how lucky I was to be dealing with these violations within twenty-four hours. Lawyers reading this might cry foul, as the accused weren't legally represented, but I wasn't represented either and it sure was enjoyable to have violations dealt with so promptly. Dream on, modern-day enforcers! The only winners in the courtroom today are the lawyers. Win or lose, both lawyers get paid. Wouldn't it be fun if only the winning lawyer got paid? I made another quick trip to La Ronge to deliver my second load in as many days to the commercial fishing plant.

1975: Summer of Greedy Fishermen

I was only in Missinipe for five weeks but the parade of over-limits continued. My boss called after a couple of weeks saying the person who owned the lodges had phoned claiming I was ruining his business. His customers were going home unhappy and some said they wouldn't return. I told my boss perhaps the fish population would be happier and healthier without them. He laughed and told me to keep up the good work. I really appreciated his support and doubled my efforts to catch more bad guys. It is so simple to get people to work hard just by supporting them in every way you can. I would remember this important lesson all my life.

Over the course of the next five weeks I caught and charged thirty-nine people, mostly Americans, for gross over-limits of all kinds of fish. I was addicted to catching poachers. Every plane I heard caused my pulse to quicken as I headed down to the docks. I was only doing this in the evening, as I had to work in the campgrounds during the day. I was having so much fun getting paid for working eight hours and getting $26.38 a day. I didn't care about overtime. I didn't even know it was possible to get paid for it. I just loved what I was doing and would have worked for less.

Only a handful of the fishermen showed any remorse for the

over-limits. It was a different time back then. Some tried to hide their catch in luggage or other bags as word got out that I might check them when they returned. Others sent their fish out ahead of them. I probably missed some, but with a large nose like mine I was able to sniff out most of the hidden cargo. At the end of my five weeks in Missinipe I made one last presentation before the JP. After the proceedings he shook my hand and congratulated me for a job well done. I made one last trip down the winding gravel road to La Ronge and delivered my last load of fish to the commercial plant and the plant manager came to greet me. He said "Randy, you've delivered more fish this summer than any commercial fisherman on Lac La Ronge." I had mixed emotions about that. It was great that I'd caught so many fishermen breaking the law but it was sad that so many were willing to break the law. Little did I know how committed I would become to catching poachers over the next thirty-six years.

There is a good ending to this story though. Thirty-seven years later, in 2012, I returned to Missinipe. I'd purchased a fly-in fishing trip that had been donated to the North American Wildlife Enforcement Officers Association convention in Saskatoon by the same lodge owner whose guest fishermen I'd charged in 1975. It would be a retirement gift to my wife and two of my children. I walked into the float-plane base in Missinipe and reintroduced myself to the lodge owner from thirty-seven years earlier. He invited my wife and me into his office and we had a great chat. He was a wonderful, funny man and over the course of our chat he came close to thanking me for what I'd done so many years ago. The fly-in camps still have great fishing and I knew from discussions with the current conservation officers that he'd changed his attitude many years ago. It was a very rewarding meeting. I have looked back on that summer of 1975 so many times and I realize how fortunate I was to have a job like that.

Running Back to Saskatoon

I returned to Saskatoon in the fall of 1975 for my second year of renewable resources training. I didn't know where I might work the next year but I did know I was hooked on poachers. My second year at Kelsey Institute was more fun than the first. Two fellow students and I managed to rent a small house. No more peanut butter and dill pickle sandwiches! We had a great time and we all excelled in class. Two of us also did great with the ladies and we both met girls we'd eventually marry. Randy Webb and I would cross career paths many times in the future and he's still a great friend with a wonderful wife.

I met my future wife, Lorraine, at a terrific event called the Keg-orama. This involved several hundred students rolling full kegs of beer down the streets of Saskatoon and ending up at the Besborough Hotel where the kegs were emptied into our waiting glasses. Lorraine approached me and I remembered her from her hometown about eighty miles from mine. Our schools had been rivals in sport but her beautiful smile quickly made me forget that they often beat us. The rest of the year breezed by. The classes were long hours and the workload was intense but the fun never ended.

I did get myself into the dean's office for a "discussion" once. One of our rival programs was called Recreation Technology, and we didn't like each other. Their course seemed rather easy compared to ours and we often said things to each other that promoted the rivalry. They took knitting! They played dodgeball! One night a friend and I decided to make a fake exam for the Recreation Technology students. We had a lot of laughs writing it. I went into the institute late that night with about ten copies of the exam and posted them on all the bulletin boards in the school.

The next morning the fan made contact with last night's dinner. The Rec. Tech. students were livid. They wanted the writer to hang. Well, maybe not hang but they were angry. Later that morning I was called to the dean's office. I was nervous. I thought I'd be kicked out. I sat down and folded my sweaty palms. The dean was looking down at a copy of the exam I'd written. He peered over his glasses and said, "Randy, I understand you wrote this." "Yes sir, I did." He paused and then continued to read the exam. He started to smile. I'd never seen this man smile. "I need to keep this in my file. Do you have another copy?" "Yes sir, I can return them all to you." I thought being honest was the best way to save my education. "No, I just need one copy because this is very funny and I'd like to have one for myself." "Are you serious?" I asked. "Yes Randy, but don't do it again. Consider this dealt with and don't discuss our meeting with anyone." I leapt out of the chair and kept my nose clean for the rest of the course. Well, except for our late-night entry into the snow sculpture contest when a few of us built a fairly large replica of part of the male anatomy on the front lawn of the college.

Upon graduation I parted ways with many very close friends. Lorraine had another year in her course so she would remain in Saskatoon. A number of provincial hiring boards came to the college to interview students for permanent and part-time work. I applied to work in Northern Saskatchewan again. I also applied for Manitoba and the Department of Fisheries and Oceans in BC. Northern Saskatchewan offered me the job first and I gladly accepted. I declined Manitoba's offer and was put on an eligible list for BC. I was asked to report to Beauval, Saskatchewan, about a three-hour drive north of Saskatoon.

Better than Turnips

I reported to Beauval in late May 1976, eager to continue hunting poachers. I worked for a great boss, Dave Coombes, and I also worked with two seasonal employees, Victor and Frank Bouvier. Victor and Frank were from a local First Nations band. They knew everyone and every lake, creek and road in the country. Victor was a very strong man with a build like Bruce Lee. He could load a forty-five-gallon drum of fuel into the back of a pickup by himself. I liked him. He made me feel safe. Officers didn't carry side arms back then and encountering unhappy armed people on remote roads was simply dangerous work. The accommodation supplied to me consisted of two small rooms in the back of the office. There wasn't any furniture in the place so I was given a budget of $200 to furnish it. I rummaged around and managed to purchase a stove, fridge, bed, table and chairs and a few other small items for the $200. I was easy to please and just happy to be working at something so enjoyable. Sure the propane stove leaked and the wind whistled through the cracks around the windows but it was home and the outdoor toilet was much better than the one on the farm! Life was good.

I was fairly naive about First Nations' issues in 1976. My only encounter with First Nations had been a Native man who was hired help on our farm when I was very young. He was a hard-working man who treated us kids well and he seemed more like an uncle than a hired hand. Anyway, I was soon to find myself in the middle of hunting controversies.

One day I took a small aluminum boat up the Beaver River for a patrol. I was by myself and I wasn't a great outdoor navigator. It was fairly simple on the river though: head upstream on the patrol and downstream to get home. All those years of schooling were paying off! I came around a bend in the river just as a shot rang out. Two Natives in a boat were about a hundred yards in front of me and they'd just taken a shot at a cow moose standing in the water near them. This was summer and not moose season but I was alone and they had a rifle. I approached them and tried to act casual even though my heart was pounding in my ears. They seemed friendly enough and we started to talk. They wanted to know if I was taking their moose. It didn't take me long to say no, as there was no way I could load the moose into my boat or tow it the ten miles with my 9.9-hp engine. Sometimes instincts take over and it's just best to follow them. I watched as they started to gut and clean the moose. They provided me with their names and other information that I recorded in my notebook.

After pulling the entrails from the moose, they rolled the pile over and pulled out one of the stomach chambers, cut it open, chopped off a piece of the stomach lining (tripe) and rinsed it off in the river. One of them stood up, cut off a small chunk and handed it to me saying, "Here, white boy, try this." I accepted his offer and gagged at the thought of eating it. I watched as each of them took a piece and began chewing it. A lot of thoughts went through my mind before I carefully placed the piece of tripe to my nose. "I've smelled worse," I said. "Better than turnips." To their surprise I put the piece in my mouth and started to chew. It wasn't that bad. It had the flavour of grass. They offered me more but I declined. I had passed the test.

I returned to the office and provided the information to my

boss but in the end no charges were laid as the two men belonged to a very remote reserve upstream and the moose would be totally consumed by those that needed it. It would be the topic of future discussions with the band, though, as shooting a cow in the summer was killing two moose at once.

Creek Poachers and the Noisy Muffler

My summer was passing quickly, with a number of charges laid to fishers for over-limits, no licence and other misdemeanours. The really "good" ones to catch were always those who had abandoned any sense of the law to take fish or wildlife, some for profit and some for greed. A fairly common, but difficult, offence to catch someone at was snaring or spearing spawning pike or walleye in creeks at night. My partner, Victor, and I really wanted to catch some of these bandits. We'd checked a creek about an hour away and had found evidence of people poaching near a bridge so we decided to come back in the middle of the night.

I met Victor at the office at 3 a.m. and we set off in our Dodge patrol vehicle toward the bridge on the creek. We were about halfway down the bumpy, winding gravel road when the muffler fell off the truck. Victor suggested we go back to the office because the poachers would hear us coming for miles, but I said, "Why don't we just drive it like this? We'll just sound like some more poachers with a crappy truck and they won't suspect anything." Victor was reluctant but agreed to drive to the bridge. As we reached it, driving fairly fast, we could see the tail lights of another vehicle so we drove right onto the bridge, stopped our truck, bailed out and shone our flashlights down into the creek. Three men were wading around with gaffs and spears, throwing walleye up onto the banks. Remarkably, they didn't stop but instead asked us to shine the light in the water for them. We did so and watched all three of them catching fish. Then Victor said, "I've think you've got enough fish, boys."

The three poachers stopped and looked up in bewilderment. "Wait your turn!" one shouted. "No," Victor replied. "We're conservation officers." The shocked poachers dropped their gaffs and came up onto the bridge. They'd obviously been drinking and were not happy. They directed their frustration at Victor as he was doing the talking, and they started becoming nasty and belligerent. Victor remained calm until one snorted, "You think you're pretty tough wearing that shirt. If you didn't have that on we'd take care of you." I'll never forget his reaction. It was like a scene from *The Incredible Hulk*. Victor clenched his teeth and fists, then ripped his shirt open, pulled it off and slammed it to the ground. He glared at the three men and said, "I don't have my shirt on now!" I was terrified, but knowing Victor could lift a forty-five-gallon drum of fuel eased my fear. The headlights shone on the chest and biceps of Victor's ripped torso. The three men did some sober reflection and calmed down, and they all co-operated as we gathered up the fish and all the gear they'd used. We gave them each an appearance notice and sent them on their way.

I drove back to Beauval with Victor wearing his shirt with holes instead of buttons. The first thing he did was to apologize for having lost his temper. I didn't accept his unnecessary apology because I thought his reaction had prevented a battle that could have gotten ugly. They had gaffs and we had nothing. From that day on, I always enjoyed being in Victor's company when things got serious.

Culture Shock: Moving to Vancouver

I t was nearly Christmas when I received a phone call from DFO in BC. They were offering me a permanent job as a fishery officer starting in Vancouver. They gave me twenty-four hours to decide. What should I do? I liked working for my boss and I loved the work. I'd only been to BC once and had never been to the coast. I'd never seen a salmon. Would I miss this place? I lay in bed watching the bitter, cold wind rustle the curtains on my window. I thought about the outdoor toilet fifty feet from my front door. I breathed in the strong scent of propane from my leaky stove. Could things get better than this? I talked to my boss the next morning and he encouraged me to go. I phoned Lorraine in Saskatoon and told her about the job I'd been offered in BC. That would be the most difficult part of accepting the job. I'd be a thousand miles away from Lorraine, but she supported me as she would over the rest of our lifetime. I called and accepted the job.

I had two weeks to move and report to work. Fortunately for me my good friend Randy Webb, with whom I'd lived in college and who had worked north of me in Saskatchewan for a while, had moved to BC shortly before I did. I called him up and we arranged to rent an apartment together in the West End of Vancouver. I packed my belongings into my pickup and drove them to the train station to be transported to BC. Lorraine drove me to the airport in Saskatoon and I left my home, my family, my friends and Lorraine behind.

My DFO Career: The First Eight Months

On my way to the DFO headquarters at 1090 West Pender Street in downtown Vancouver I stood on the corner of one intersection and looked up. The walk light changed twice before I caught myself staring skyward at the mountains of buildings. I was a long ways from "Hodgeville, Sask."

I couldn't believe how many forms I had to fill out. Paperwork makes the world go around — and around and around. I was shown my desk in the Operations Room. I was to be a radio operator/call centre/information centre all in one. I quickly settled into the busy routines of sending out fishing notices and responding to public inquires but I must apologize to some of you who may have called in asking for fishing information back then. You probably didn't know I had never been on the ocean or seen a salmon and yet there I was, providing all the latest tips on where to go. I had to call many people back once I'd tracked down the answer.

I remember receiving a call asking how the chuck fishing was. I paused and said, "I'm not sure but I'll get the latest information and call you back." I hung up and began looking through all the books I had. What was chuck fishing? I'd heard of hootchies, trolling, mooching and jigging but I'd never heard of this. I went to find an answer and was ridiculed with laughter when I asked what chuck fishing was. It was simply slang for fishing in salt water. This job was tough! I was treated with patience and tried to learn fast. I knew this was a test for me and that fieldwork would be my reward.

All the new fishery officers were asked to provide a summary of their first six to eight months with DFO. I was somewhat taken aback by the bureaucracy and how decisions were made but I liked to find some humour in life and so I wrote the following account of my first eight months. When I look back and read it today I wonder how I held the job. It wouldn't pass today's standards of professional behaviour. Throughout my career I've kept many documents that meant something to me. Why I kept them for over thirty-five years some may question but some things are worth keeping and if it wasn't for packrats like me there wouldn't be any museums.

My Fisheries Career

My Fisheries career began on January 24, 1977, when I touched down at Vancouver International Airport in heavy fog. A Fisheries employee who escorted me to 1090 West Pender Street, more locally known as the Ivory Tower, greeted me. I cautiously entered the elevator and pushed number 7. The person to whom I was to report had recently retired so I was directed to the 10th floor where a sign read "On Holidays." The next sign read "Out to Lunch." An appropriate phrase, I thought. After several more stops I ended up back on the 7th floor where I'd started. Little did I know how habit forming this routine was to become.

After a short briefing I was sent across the street to sign forms and forms and more forms. A few pens later I returned to the 8th floor of 1090 where I'd heard I'd be working and, needless to say, my boss was on holidays. But I was not alone; a clerk with three days' experience was there to help. I began work immediately, answering insulting phone calls and ignorant letters and filing mountains of paper. The complex filing system was difficult to grasp at first, but through keen observation of other employees I soon got the idea; flip a coin. After

The FPV Surge Rock *was a classic wooden patrol vessel, one of dozens that used to patrol the West Coast into the 1970s.*

a few weeks I was sent to be measured for a uniform; I promptly received it seven months later.

In May I was informed I'd be stationed in River's Inlet. In a few weeks I'd forwarded all my belongings and was ready for the big step into the field. But I ended up off Langara Island on an offshore patrol on the Fisheries Patrol Vessel (FPV) *Howay.* I had a wonderful time although the first few days were spent hanging over the rail and feeding the gulls. Upon my return to Vancouver, still eager for River's Inlet, I was told my destination would be Bella Coola. Two hours later I was told Bella Bella. The next day the decision had been returned to Bella Coola. Before any further changes were made I jumped the next Goose (airplane) and headed to Bella Coola even though my belongings were now in River's Inlet. An expense claim for the move was submitted and I promptly received payment 122 days later.

After roaming Dean Channel on the FPV *Temple Rock* for a month I was sent to Bella Bella. This time I was fortunate enough to be given twenty-four hours notice. I was enjoying the country on the FPV *Surge Rock* when a call came in from Vancouver to proceed to Prince Rupert. I was picked up by aircraft and rushed to Bella Bella, where I packed in twenty minutes and was off to Rupert. No explanation. No warning. No travel advance. Upon arrival I was given a car and told to proceed to Smithers to get instructions from the fishery officer there. He was on holidays. I blindly proceeded to patrol the Moricetown Food Fishery, which nearly led to the Moricetown Massacre. Two weeks changed to four before I returned to Bella Bella. My thoughts as I landed in Bella Bella were, "Settled at last." Two hours later I was off to River's Inlet to work there for an unspecified period and here I am, right where I was to be sent eight months ago.

Although this satirical memo was critical of DFO, the department truly was a great organization to work for. I'm sure similar things happen in most large organizations. I do, however, hold a record that is unlikely ever to be broken; I worked out of fourteen locations in my first year of employment as a fishery officer.

My First and Only Offshore Patrol

In early June of 1977 I was told I'd be going on an offshore patrol checking Japanese longline fishing boats, as Canada had recently created a twelve-mile limit. My patrol partner would be Randy Webb. I had never been on the ocean before, and when my feet hit land seventeen days later I promised myself to avoid such an experience ever again. The first three days at sea were fairly rough and I was seasick for that entire time. I was getting weak because I couldn't even drink water. The skipper had just decided to take me in when I suddenly snapped out of it and I have rarely been seasick since.

Randy and I boarded and checked a number of Japanese vessels and upon completion of our inspections there was always an exchange of gifts. I'd been told the most appreciated gift would be a few *Playboy* magazines. One *Playboy* was exchanged for three litres of sake, which I thought was a good trade until I tasted sake!

Our patrol continued north to Prince Rupert, where the boat tied up overnight. Randy and I joined the crew and headed to the bar. We returned to the boat late but a number of the crewmen hadn't returned by morning. It turned out a few of them had had way too much to drink and had got in an argument. Three crew members had allegedly made racist comments to another crew member who had walked away and quit. When the three crewmen returned to the boat and told the skipper what happened they were fired on the spot.

The skipper advised everyone the boat was leaving Prince Rupert, and he told Randy and me we'd have to take turns steering the ship because he'd left a few crew behind. Neither of us had ever done this but we seemed to be doing okay—until the weather turned very ugly offshore. Huge waves were breaking over the bow of the 120-foot vessel with such force the whole wheelhouse shuddered. Everyone was scared. The vessel was rocking so violently from side to side that oil was being forced out the sides of the engines. No one was allowed outside for fear of being swept overboard. Steering the large ship was a challenge in the high winds and seas, and it was a tiring workout. The skipper kept reminding us not to get the ship turned sideways or we'd flip. The pucker factor was very high on that trip but we made it through. It was one of those times when I thought a snowstorm with temperatures of 30 below would have been a better place to be.

The polished brass in the wheelhouse of the FPV Howay still glistens, even as the 120-foot ship is tossed around in the heavy seas off the BC coast.

The weather improved the next day. Our trip south to Vancouver continued and Randy and I were told to check some commercial trollers off the west coast of Vancouver Island. Randy was the expert between us because he'd at least seen salmon. The salmon I'd been closest to came out of a can. We were expected to identify all five species of salmon on the boats and we had to be especially watchful for coho, because they were banned at the time. Randy and I came up with a plan. He would go down into the hold of the boats and dig through the iced-down fish looking for coho. He didn't sound real confident about it but I didn't know a sockeye from a halibut. We boarded a couple of vessels and all seemed to go well. The crews were happy to see us and treated us well, but as we left the second boat the skipper pointed across the water and said, "You really should go check that boat out." Randy and I hopped into our twelve-foot wooden boat and headed for the "bad guy." Our boarding was not welcome and we struggled to get tied up to the moving boat. Once aboard, Randy went below deck to look through the iced-down catch. He flung one salmon onto the deck and said, "Check that one out." I thought, "So that's what a salmon looks like." I picked it up and tried to appear like this was not the first salmon I'd ever handled. The fisherman scoffed at me and said, "That's a sockeye, you idiot." I said the light wasn't that good down below. The same thing happened twice more and he became more disgusted each time. When the fourth fish hit the deck I was watching the fisherman out the corner of my eye. His shoulders slumped slightly and he didn't say anything. "That's a coho!" I surmised. "Yes it is," he scowled. Randy continued digging through the hold, finding more questionable fish buried under the legal catch, and using the one fish for comparison I was now able to identify the coho. The fisherman was given an appearance notice and he had no idea these were the first salmon I'd ever seen. He later pleaded guilty to the charges.

Central Coast Pinball

On June 21, 1977, my twenty-first birthday, I was given a change of address. In one day I was told I'd be going to River's Inlet, Bella Bella and Bella Coola, and I ended up bouncing around the Central Coast like a pinball for the summer. I worked in Bella Bella, a unique part of the BC coast, for most of July and August, and DFO supplied housing on the shore directly across from the First Nations community. I was working with Randy Brahniuk and Randy Webb, so you can imagine the confusion whenever anyone phoned and asked for Randy. We ended up going by One, Two and Three. I was Number Three as I had the least experience.

Working the commercial fishery in Bella Bella resulted in the detection of a number of fishing violations. Commercial fishermen reminded me a lot of Saskatchewan farmers; no matter how good the season, there was always something to complain about, especially the government. One day Randy Two and I were on a patrol of Milbanke Sound checking commercial gillnetters, and as we approached one boat we saw fish being thrown from the deck. We tried to get alongside but the boat didn't slow down. We tried to retrieve some of the fish that were being thrown over. This wasn't a case of catch and release because we could see they had been gutted, but all the fish sank before we could retrieve them.

When we finally pulled alongside and jumped onto the boat the skipper was belligerent and rather cocky, as he'd thrown all the illegal fish overboard—or so he thought. He'd missed one and that was enough for us. We would never charge someone for one fish but we knew that he'd thrown several dozen overboard and he knew we weren't happy. He settled down and became more reasonable. Just as we were preparing to leave the boat we noticed some smoke coming from the engine hatch. What proved to be a serious electrical fire was finally extinguished, but not before his boat was totally disabled. We towed the vessel into Bella Bella where the costly repairs could be made. Sometimes justice is served outside the courtroom.

One of many stops in the summer of 1977 was Moricetown, some twenty miles northwest of Smithers. After a flight from Bella Bella to Prince Rupert I was given a car and told to drive to Smithers and report to the officer in charge. DFO was having problems with First Nations gaffing fish in a closed time (the fishery was closed two days a week) and wasting pink salmon. Sockeye, coho, chinook, steelhead trout and pink salmon were all migrating through Moricetown on the Bulkley River at the same time. The pinks were considered less desirable. The fishery took place in a raging canyon where fishers stood precariously and reached into the water with twenty-foot gaff poles. When they felt a fish, they impaled it with the gaff hook and then tried to retrieve it. Many of the pierced fish wriggled off, and those that happened to be pink salmon were usually hurled back into the river, often bouncing off the rocks on the way, because the fishers didn't want them. Many were simply thrown onto the rocks to die. The sight sickened me. (Fortunately things are much better today with the local band using dip nets and beach seines to catch most of their fish, allowing the release of non-targeted species. A much smaller gaff fishery is still allowed. Legal sales have also been negotiated with DFO, allowing some fish to be sold in years of greater abundance. The band also works with DFO to tag and release fish, to better understand migration timing and run sizes.)

At the Smithers office I met the seasonal officer I'd be working with and learned he'd been attacked and beaten the week before my arrival; he welcomed my support. My first trip into the canyon went well. It was risky work, scrambling across slippery rocks to talk and confiscate fishing gear, but people listened and backed away from me when I asked them to. They seemed more co-operative than I expected and I couldn't work out why until I discovered that the officer had told many of the fishermen I was some kind of "strongman" being brought in to clean things up. Day after day the game of cat and mouse took place with me seizing dozens of gaffs and jigs, but anxiety levels were rising because they were running out of gaffs.

Many of the fishers were young kids and I wasn't sure what to do with them, so I decided to try something. Rotting, smelly pink salmon were piled in cracks and crevices among the rocks and the stench made me gag. I took a metal bucket from the trunk of my car and each time I caught a minor fishing I made him fill the bucket with rotting fish and carry it up the steep hill to a garbage can. I would then drive the kid home to his parents and let them know what I'd done. The children's parents supported my actions because they didn't agree with wasting fish either, and the scale of the waste was huge. One day I sat on a hill overlooking the canyon, with binoculars, and I counted over 5,000 pink salmon gaffed and thrown on the bank or back into the river. The department never reported my observations but I know the number was accurate. Perhaps it was the politics and controversy they were trying to avoid.

One morning I walked out onto the bridge to observe a couple of people fishing below and the next thing I knew fifteen very angry men had surrounded me and begun pushing me, threatening to throw me in the river. I was unarmed and untrained in enforcement at the time, but no training could have prepared me for this. I tried to remain calm and reason with them. Some were intoxicated but most were just angry. I don't really know how long I was there; it felt like an eternity.

Someone in the village must have seen the ruckus and called the RCMP. When a single RCMP officer drove onto the bridge I felt relieved, but only for a minute. Someone yelled, "This guy is trying to take away our right to fish." The officer looked at them, pointed at me and said, "Well that's the guy you have to talk to," and drove away. I was shocked! I have called for and been given outstanding support from the RCMP a number of times but not on this day. Like any organization, they have incompetent employees too. The crowd stayed and I continued talking and talking because that was all I had. One by one they went away and eventually I was able to get to my car. It was one of many terrifying days I would experience throughout my career.

The next day things seemed back to normal and I continued to check fishers with renewed enthusiasm. Why would I have renewed enthusiasm after a day like that? Well, Lorraine had phoned me from Saskatoon to let me know she was coming by train to visit me in Smithers. She arrived two days later. I still had to work during her visit, because that's what I thought I had to do, and on her second day in Smithers, which happened to be her birthday, I decided to take her to Moricetown under cover. I borrowed my boss's personal truck and drove out to the canyon. No one suspected the yellow Toyota truck and I wasn't in uniform so she and I walked out onto the bridge like any other tourists would. I watched several people fishing, people I'd caught several times and suspected of selling fish, so I went down, took the gaffs from two of them, returned to the truck and placed the gaffs in the back. I asked Lorraine to watch them for me. (This is against any policy or practice of any enforcement today.) I was going down the other side of the bridge to get the other gaffs when I heard some noise up on the bridge and saw Lorraine surrounded by a group of very angry women. They were yelling racial obscenities at her and threatening her but she stood her ground and verbally knocked them back. Wow! I must marry that woman! I quickly grabbed the remaining gaffs and ran up to the truck. We left the bridge and I didn't take her back again. The next day I asked Lorraine to marry me and she accepted. I was rewarded with her unwavering support through the most difficult of times. She was DFO's most valuable unpaid employee.

Vancouver Waterfront and Chasing Crabbers

The Vancouver waterfront became my first permanent posting. In the 1970s most of the waterfront consisted of fish plants and commercial fishing docks, and I worked with two infamous older officers, Carl Kennedy and Max Tscharre. These two provided great training for many new fishery officers. Carl was the iron-fisted officer in charge and Max was the seasonal officer who could find illegal crabs wherever he looked.

One day Carl asked me to accompany him to check a groundfish dragger. Carl and I climbed the ladder down onto the deck of the boat. The skipper came running out of the wheelhouse yelling and screaming at Carl. I didn't know that the skipper and Carl had some history. It seems they had both come to Canada after the Second World War—and hadn't been on the same side. The war of words escalated quickly. Soon they were nose to nose and really providing entertainment to a group of dockworkers and myself. When Carl poked the skipper in the chest with his finger and told him we were checking his catch, the skipper lost it. The veins on his neck popped out and his eyes were lasered in on Carl, who did the sensible thing. He ran around behind me and continued his verbal challenges, wagging his finger at the skipper over my shoulder. No, actually it was under my arm, because Carl wasn't very tall.

Now I was part of the entertainment too. I asked the skipper if I could talk to him and he calmed down a bit. Carl said I could take care of this case from here on. "Gee thanks," I thought. The skipper was fairly co-operative from that point on. I later realized that both of them were simply reacting to some horrible things that had happened to them in the war. The boat had more illegal fish on board than could be tolerated so charges were laid. He was convicted at trial, given a fine and forfeiture of the fish. After that, when I saw that boat tied to the dock I tried to make sure I checked it by myself.

Many new officers spent time with Max chasing illegal crabbers throughout the Vancouver area. It was sheer sport. Many of the offenders were immigrants but they knew they were breaking the law; they just couldn't resist free seafood. Max had his "trap line" of docks to check and we'd often head out late at night. The extremes that people would go to to hide the crabs was amazing; we found crabs hidden in the bushes, under floorboards, in the trunk, in a purse—nothing would surprise us. I think Max's favourite was the night we approached three people in Cates Park in North Vancouver. They were returning to their car carrying two traps and they seemed nervous. As we stood there questioning them, one was especially nervous. He was shifting from side to side almost like a child who had to go to the bathroom. Then he suddenly yelled, "Ouch!" and clutched his groin. It turned out he had five under-sized crabs (of the ocean variety) in his pockets and one had bitten him right near the jewellery.

One night at a dock on Jericho Beach I approached a group of five people crab fishing. They didn't see me coming and I was right beside them before I identified myself and told them to pull their traps up. They all ignored me. I asked again. Still nothing. After the third request I said, "Are you guys deaf? Pull up your traps!"

Then I tapped one of them on the shoulder. He seemed startled and started giving me sign language—not the single-digit sign language that I often saw, but sign language for the deaf. Oh I felt bad. They were a group of kids from the school for the deaf. I pointed to the sign on the dock and they all started signing each other. One pulled out a notepad and wrote, "We're sorry, we didn't see the sign in the dark." I wasn't sure I totally believed them but I sent them on their way. Another late night on the same dock I approached two Asian males. They had twenty or thirty very small Dungeness crabs in buckets. This would not be a warning. I took them to my vehicle and began to take a statement from one of them as he pleaded with me, "First time. Just warning." I had heard those words so many times before I had to try not to laugh. He leaned over, put his head on my shoulder and pretended to cry. People would try anything but this guy needed remedial acting lessons.

One of my favourite crab cases involved a seafood store in Chinatown. We would routinely check seafood stores for size limits and receipts for fish products. We walked into this place and went to the live crab tank. A number of them appeared to be small so we called the owner over. He was a small, slightly built man, probably in his fifties. As is often the case, language became an issue. He forgot we'd been into the store before and knew he could speak English. We pointed to the crab tank and our measuring device. We measured the crabs and removed the undersized ones, and now the little man flipped. He ran around the store waving his arms in the air and yelling. I don't know any Cantonese, but I don't think he was inviting us to stay for tea.

People in the store were looking at us. I'm sure they thought we were taking him away. It was hard not to smile as he tore around the place. Then he ran around the counter, pulled several of the remaining crabs from the live tank and ran out front of his store to a metal garbage can. In his verbal rage he slammed them one by one into the bottom of the empty metal can. Running back inside, he got some more and proceeded to slam them into the garbage can as well. Max and I started to laugh. When was the *Candid Camera* going to show up? Next the store owner climbed into the garbage can and began stomping on the legally measured crabs, yelling at the top of his lungs. After about two minutes he stopped, climbed out of the garbage can and went back into the store. Max and I looked into the can at the pile of mush he'd made. We walked back into the store where the owner had calmed down. Having released his frustrations he was very co-operative with us while we gave him his paperwork, and his knowledge of English mysteriously returned.

Jericho Beach dock was a staple on Max's trap line. One night we approached a group of four young men pulling crab traps. We'd been watching them for about an hour and knew they'd all fished and had kept everything they'd caught. This would be a fairly ordinary charge — but with Vancouver crab fishermen nothing is ordinary. As we approached them they hurried into a huddle like a group of goslings. I identified myself and asked them for their identification. "No English! No English!" they all chimed in. It really can be difficult to determine whether people honestly can't speak English but I came up with a plan. I got the four men to stand close to me in a circle. I began to show them how to measure a crab and I pointed to the closure sign. They were constantly talking in Cantonese. Then I pointed into the bucket of crabs and all four looked down into the bucket. As they were staring into the bucket I said, "Does anybody here understand the word *deportation?*" Two of them snapped their heads in my direction. I said, "I'll talk to the two of you because you can speak English." They co-operated from that point on, realizing they'd been had.

The freighters in Vancouver harbour and those outside Vancouver frequently waited for days, or even weeks, to be loaded, and the crews on board would often hang crab traps over the side of the ships. This was illegal, but it was not worth going through the hassle of boarding a ship and trying to determine who'd set the traps. It was much easier to simply cut the ropes and seize the traps.

This became a game for those who continued to set traps. We'd race up in our speedboat, grab the line and cut it to retrieve the trap. Sometimes the crew would be frantically pulling the lines as we approached. We didn't miss many that we went after and it was usually quite entertaining, and challenging, trying to get to the traps first. Our best haul was twenty-seven traps on one patrol. For those traps that we pulled when no one was present we'd tie our business card on the end of the rope. No one ever called us back.

The Bumper Car Bust

Some of the fishing spots we checked were very dark and away from the city lights. Max and I checked such a location in Burnaby one night. We had to walk about a half mile to one spot. As we got closer we could see the silhouettes of two people on a dock. We slowly crept closer using trees for cover and got right to the dock without them seeing us. They had nowhere to go so we quickly approached, identified ourselves and had their traps and buckets before they knew what had happened. The two were very co-operative—almost too co-operative.

We were halfway to our car when one of them started running away. I yelled at Max to stay with the other guy and the evidence while I caught him. This was my first foot chase. I was fairly fit at the time and had started to run three or four times a week. I caught him easily but then he started to struggle. This was a lesson I would remember. In future chases (and there were lots of them) I'd never try to catch the poacher right away. Run until they are tired, then run them some more. Once they were totally exhausted I'd arrest them without incident. I never again had a struggle with anyone I chased. Back to this runner I'd caught. He struggled to get away but I was able to handle this jockey-sized sprinter and I managed to get him in handcuffs just as Max and the other guy arrived.

The one provided us with his proper identification but the one I'd chased didn't have any. My instincts told me to take him into the closest police station but we ended up believing his story and wrote all the information down. The two men were to appear in court a month later but only the guy who had produced the identification showed up, and he pleaded not guilty. His lawyer said the other guy had caught all the crabs and his client didn't know who he was. A warrant was issued but I knew I'd been scammed by a false name. That one really bugged me because I am usually very thorough.

Months passed and it still was getting to me but I knew I'd probably never see the man again among the two or three million people in the Lower Mainland. I'd nearly forgotten about the case with all the other action going on until one Saturday night the following summer when a few friends and I decided it was time for another night at Playland. Such nights usually consisted of a round of minigolf, a roller-coaster ride and my favourite, Banging Beavers (or Whack-a-mole as it later became known). I'd win enough rounds for a large bear before the carny cut me off. We were ready to leave when someone suggested a round of bumper cars. I tucked my bear in beside me and the games began. It felt just like driving in downtown Vancouver: everyone driving in circles yelling at each other. I lined up a direct hit on an unsuspecting man and my car bounced off his side before he saw me. That felt good! He turned to look at me and I knew this was the crab fisherman that had provided me with false information. I bounced him a few more times before the ride ended and then I walked up to him with my teddy bear under my arm and pulled out my badge. Busted on a bumper car! He didn't run this time and provided me with his driver's licence. My friends stood nearby laughing so loud I think the guy was getting annoyed. Too bad for him! "Don't mess with a fishery officer," I thought. I'm fairly certain I am the only officer in history that arrested someone on a bumper car. I walked him back to his vehicle to get information from it as well. Then I called another officer to bring me some paperwork and I issued it to him. The courts treated him appropriately—$1,000 fine for the crabs and providing false information.

The Naked Truth

Anyone who spends a lot of time in the outdoors has probably encountered naked people doing whatever naked people in the outdoors might do. It's one of the hazards of the job. Such a sight can range anywhere from funny to nauseous. Wreck Beach was and still is a nudist beach, and people used to be allowed to catch smelts (small herring-like fish) there and along English Bay. I did as any keen young officer would do and that was to patrol whenever and wherever I had to, and I'll always remember my first patrol of Wreck Beach.

Another officer and I were asked to check out the smelt fishermen one afternoon. We walked out onto the beach (in full uniform of course) and proceeded along the shoreline. I was a fairly shy person at the time so it felt a bit awkward talking to naked people. (Where do you look? You can only look into their eyes for so long before they think you are a bit strange.) The first group had a licence and all checked out fine. The second group was the other extreme—no licence, too long a net and too many fish. The three of them seemed a bit taken aback at being checked. A fourth person nearby walked up to me and flashed his Vancouver Police Department badge. (I'm still not sure where he pulled that badge from.) The naked man stood there holding his badge and said, "They're okay, they're with me." I couldn't believe anyone would have the "balls" to try "flashing" his badge while standing completely naked. I told him I didn't think he wanted to be part of their group as they were going to be charged. He folded up his badge, turned the other cheeks and walked away.

A second naked story took place under fairly unusual circumstances as well. Another officer and I were sent to the Queen Charlotte Islands (Haida Gwaii) to board and check commercial fishing boats. We worked off a larger patrol boat with a twelve-foot wooden boat. We checked a number of vessels and found several without licences and committing other minor violations; where patrols are infrequent people tend to ignore the rules. We boarded a troller on the second day and were greeted by a seemingly polite, law-abiding fisherman. Everything checked out until we asked if he had anyone else on board. He directed us to his cabin and said his friend was inside. The other officer stepped down into the cabin and I stayed in the doorway. The person appeared to be sleeping so we told them who we were and said we wanted to check their licence. The person quickly sat up and the covers fell down to reveal a naked female. We both turned away expecting her to cover herself up but she just sat there smiling at us. The other officer left it to me to gather information from her before we departed. I guess he thought my experiences on Wreck Beach had helped prepare me for this. We gave her a warning for not having a commercial licence and scored her a nine for her outstanding smile.

Lost and Found

The work in Vancouver included using a twenty-foot fibreglass patrol boat. One sunny fall day I boarded the boat alone to patrol Howe Sound to check recreational and commercial fishers. Policies today don't allow single officer patrols but back then patrolling alone was not uncommon.

It was the middle of the afternoon, I'd caught a few fishers with illegal catch and I began to work my way back to Vancouver. What I'd failed to notice was a fast-moving fog bank coming in from the west. Within minutes I was surrounded by thick fog with zero visibility.

The first thought when fog closes in is not just "Where am I?" It's more important to know where other vessels are, especially large ones such as ferries and tugboats. I throttled back and watched the very erratic "Crackerjack" compass spin wildly. The boat wasn't equipped with radar and the compass was virtually useless.

I took an educated guess and directed the boat toward where I thought I'd last seen the shore. I planned to find the shoreline of West Vancouver and work my way along the beach back to Vancouver. After about fifteen minutes of travel I realized I probably hadn't gone in the right direction. I wasn't too concerned because I had lots of fuel. My biggest concern was that I might have to call a patrol boat to come find me. I'd never live down the ribbing about my Saskatchewan navigation skills.

Then I saw something directly ahead of me. It was another boat! Great! I could get help from them as they had radar. As I moved closer I realized it was a commercial troller. That was even better news because he was likely to be heading into Vancouver and I could follow him. Then another surprise hit me. He had his fishing lines out and was trolling! The area hadn't been open to trolling in years. I quickly forgot about being lost and turned my attention to the boat in front of me.

I came alongside the troller and ordered him to pull in his gear and stop the boat. He complied and I tied up to him and jumped aboard. "How did you find me? You don't even have radar on that thing," he queried. My quick response was, "We have our ways."

The fisherman was so impressed he co-operated fully. I seized some of his gear and the fish on board. We then sat down at his galley table and I took a statement from him. I kept thinking about how I would ask him to help me back to port. My statement kept getting longer than necessary as we drifted quietly in the fog. My questions included, "Do you know where you are fishing?" "Yes," he replied. "Can you show me your radar is working?" This question was for two reasons: to prove his navigation was working but also to allow me to see where I was. He showed me the radar and I could see we were still some way from the North Shore. Then my wishes were answered!

A slight break in the fog exposed a familiar part of the coast. I quickly finished my statement and headed out. The skipper helped push my boat away from him as I left and looking in through the window he shook his head. "You don't even have a proper compass! I can't believe it." I just smiled and waved and thanked my lucky stars. No one else had to know.

Roe, Roe, Roe in Your Boat!

J oe Chambers, a new fishery officer, and I were sent to Tofino in late February of 1978 for the roe herring fishery. We were to board a seine boat chartered by the department to echo-sound and sample herring stocks for roe maturity. Herring are fished for the roe from the female herring and the goal was to catch them at the peak of their maturity just before they spawned when they had the highest percent of roe by body weight.

The first week was interesting as everything was new. We were learning how to read the sounding paper to estimate total stocks and how to test the maturity of the herring. By March 4 things started getting even more interesting. Commercial seine boats and gillnetters were showing up in big numbers. The test results were climbing and the fishery looked to be a good one. The fishery back then was a derby style where everyone caught as much as they could during the opening. The trick for DFO was to estimate when to close the fishery so the quota wouldn't be exceeded.

To complicate things further the quota had to be split between gillnetters and seine boats. The seine boats were capable of catching hundreds of tons in a single set, worth over a million dollars. The gillnets caught fish at a more predictable, controlled rate. The pressure on the fishermen and the pressure they put on DFO staff was high.

The fishery started out okay but then the weather made a sudden change for the worse. Gillnet punts were sinking and larger boats were being blown onto the rocks. The winds were so strong they blew the cups off our patrol boat's wind speed indicator. I saw my first smoke on the water—the wind blowing water droplets into the air so it looked like smoke. It was a mess. The good news was no one was killed.

The lucrative fishery was causing fishermen to take risks. There was pressure to close the fishery for safety reasons but others insisted the fishery be left open. In the end some areas were left open and others were closed.

The fishery finally ended as successfully as possible given the weather. Most of the time had been spent helping rescue fishermen and pulling in gillnets that had come loose and washed up on the beach. Those were long days on very rough seas and after three weeks on the water I was more than ready to get my feet on land.

Despite a stormy start, Joe and I developed a strong friendship and he worked for the DFO for the rest of his life.

Return to Vancouver

T hen it was back to Vancouver for more fun with crab fishermen and fish plants and patrolling Howe Sound looking for bad guys. Most of the job was enjoyable although some days, not so much. One of those days occurred on July 18, 1978. I was called at 1:30 a.m. and told to get to Lillooet right away. There were problems with the aboriginal fishery and they needed as many officers as possible.

I drove to Lillooet and called on the radio to announce my arrival. I had not yet received enforcement training in Regina because DFO had only just started sending officers through training. My turn would come after they'd trained the more senior officers. I was sent to meet another group of new untrained officers.

We sat in the hills overlooking Lillooet as the sun rose. The traffic on our VHF radios was busy and the confrontation was escalating. Natives were fishing in Bridge River rapids on the Fraser River during the closed time and had challenged DFO on the closure. The officers who were sent in to pull nets were met with large numbers of very angry people. The local federal member of Parliament was among them and he was arrested along with a number of others. Amazingly no one fell into the river and cooler heads did eventually prevail.

Back in Vancouver another Native issue was heating up. Members of the local band near the Capilano River were building rock dams across the low flow of the river to stop salmon from migrating upstream to the hatchery. They were gaffing the stranded fish below the dams and I was told to remove the dams and charge those caught fishing.

The dams were two feet high and over a hundred feet long in places. I spent many hours tearing down the dams only to see them rebuilt overnight. This went on day after day. All those rock-picking skills on the farm were paying off! I began to form my own opinion about some of the issues I was being thrown into. I thought that simply doing something because the law was on our side might not always be the best long-term solution. I was learning, but I wasn't able to change the system in the short term. The rock building and dismantling carried on for weeks until the salmon run was over.

Dismantling the large dams built by local fishers to trap migrating salmon on the Capilano River in West Vancouver reminded me of my rock-picking days from the farm.

Patrolling Howe Sound was always eventful. In the 1970s American sports fishermen came to BC in great numbers to catch our plentiful salmon, taking advantage of our liberal possession limits. Many brought canners and set up camps, especially in the Campbell River area. This was creating a conflict with Canadian fishermen. As fishery officers, we focused our attention on the greedy ones regardless of where they were from.

One Monday morning I headed to the office to check my inbox and I picked up an envelope with postage marks completely covering both sides of it. I opened it to find one of my pay cheques from over a year earlier. I had moved so many times the envelope had been lost trying to catch up to me. I hadn't even missed the cheque because I was having so much fun working and travelling around. I still have the envelope.

Weeks flew by as the summer passed and the work continued to bring new challenges and fun. I was making frequent calls back to Lorraine as our wedding date of October 14 was fast approaching. My good friend Randy Webb and I had chosen wedding dates one week apart so we could attend each other's weddings in Saskatchewan.

After our wedding Lorraine and I returned to Vancouver and started our "happily ever after" in a small wartime home in North Vancouver but then we decided to do what many new fishery officers and families did early in their careers, and that was to head north.

Terrace Bound

I applied for a vacant position and in 1979 we relocated to Terrace. I worked with a couple of wonderful officers, John Hipp and George Kofoed, who were born and raised in Terrace. They were more than willing to share their knowledge and provided a whole new world of poacher chasing.

George had been a logger for twenty-five years before joining DFO. He also trapped. His knowledge of the area, people and logging industry made him a wealth of information that I was fortunate enough to learn from. Both of them had a great sense of humour. John was well known for his old one-liners, such as: lower than a snake's belly in a wagon rut; smiling like a coyote dragging guts from a brush pile; hornier than a three-peckered hoot owl; colder than a well digger's heel; darker than the inside of a cow.

John wasn't as good at selecting an office administrator as he was at remembering good one-liners though, at least not the first time. I walked into the office one day to find the lady he had hired clipping her dirty toenails on the keyboard and letting the pieces fall between the keys. Had it not been for the fact that she lacked personal hygiene (aside from neatly clipped toenails), couldn't type and was very lazy, she might have been okay. Fortunately, the

Fishery officer George Kofoed of Terrace takes a break from navigating the tricky waters on the gorgeous Gitnadoix River valley during our patrol.

replacement administrator he hired was the top of the scale and kept us all in line.

I continued to run for fitness in Terrace and joined the local running club. I was running longer and getting faster and I soon learned that being very fit could be a huge asset when catching poachers.

I patrolled the Copper River canyon often, as it was closed to salmon fishing. The canyon was a narrow, fast-flowing section where fish would pile up before proceeding farther upstream. It was accessible only via a very steep trail dropping about 200 feet in elevation. One fall day I pulled into a wide spot on the road above the canyon and noticed a truck parked on another pullout. I took my binoculars out and made my way to several vantage points where I could look down into the canyon and not be seen from below. I saw one person by the river catching and keeping coho so I started to make my way down the trail, careful to avoid rolling any rocks down the hill. About ten minutes later I was directly above the guy and I watched him catch another coho and take it into the bush. I let him resume fishing and then approached him. I have to admit it's gratifying to tap someone on the shoulder when they don't expect it. He jumped and turned around.

During our conversation he admitted he knew the canyon was closed but he'd just arrived and hadn't caught anything. It was a response I was getting used to. In all the years of catching people there have only been a few who admitted guilt right away. It really made you develop mistrust with nearly everyone you approached. I took a statement from him and told him he was being charged for fishing in a closed area and for keeping coho. He acted surprised until I walked over to his stash and found eight coho averaging between seven and eight pounds. His head dropped and he admitted they were all his.

I told him the fishing rod, gear and fish were all being seized. He said, "Well if you're taking them all, you can pack them all out." (Note to self: It's better to tell people their fate at the truck after they've helped pack the fish out.) I quickly considered my options. I had nothing to put the fish in and they weighed between fifty and sixty pounds, but then I had an idea!

I pulled out my knife and cut two branches off a tree, each about three feet long with one shorter branch sticking out at the bottom. I fed the sticks through the gills of the fish until I had four on each one. I thought, "Now for some fun," and said, "I hope you can keep up!" I put the rod under my arm, grabbed a stick in each hand, held his tackle box on one side and started up the steep trail as fast as I could go.

I knew the guy was behind me because I could hear his breathing getting louder and louder. I was having fun. "Don't get too far behind me sir!" I said. By the time we reached the top the poor guy looked ready to pass out, with sweat dripping from his forehead and his face bright red.

Grateful to my marathon training, I took a deep breath and started talking to him without showing any sign of being short of breath. He gave me a puzzled look and said, between gasps, "What are you? How did you do that? You're not even breathing heavy!" I just smiled and told him if he'd helped me I would have walked more slowly.

Fishy Stories

One day during the summer George and I were watching some fishing sites during a closed sockeye time. We saw a family fishing and recognized them from previous encounters. We watched them pack up their fish in the trunk of their car and leave the site. George and I jumped into our truck and followed them. This guy had been known to illegally sell fish in the past. He turned down a road leading to his residence and George turned the red lights on. The car didn't stop. He turned the siren on. The old driver jumped up in his seat, swerved to the right and hit two huge potholes. Everyone in the car was bouncing around like Ping-Pong balls. He pulled to a stop and dust poured out the windows from the inside of the car as the occupants stumbled out onto the road. No one was hurt but the driver was unhappy.

I started hearing unpleasant names again. My name tag is quite visible on my shirt, so why do people insist on calling me so many other names? I would eventually learn that the name-calling was generally not aimed at me but at the organization and the society I represented. That made it easier to understand but certainly didn't help diffuse these tense situations.

We calmed the old guy down until we said we wanted to look in his trunk. Off he went again. He finally relented and opened the trunk. No fish! George reached into the trunk and pulled the car jack out, lifted the floor and found fifteen fresh sockeye. Everyone complied from that point on.

The next day I received a phone call from Vancouver about a complaint filed by the older man. He claimed that we'd run him off the road and George had threatened to hit him with the jack. I couldn't believe it. This was so far from reality.

In the following days the man's band went to the media and all media outlets in the province were covering the story—only the one side of

It was gratifying to find streams filled with 60-plus-pound spawned out Chinook salmon while walking the Kalum River near Terrace in 1979.

course. It took days of writing notes and answering calls. Months passed before the "fish story" faded away. Eventually a trial took place and the man was convicted. It was another lesson for me in the real world. The media only print what they know, and in court cases the officers cannot comment until the trial is over. In later years I learned to educate the media ahead of time. They will usually publish the facts when given a chance.

I was on a patrol alone one afternoon and checking fishing sites around town in Terrace. The river was closed at the time. I drove across the wooden bridge over the Skeena River and noticed two people fishing with a gillnet just upstream of the bridge. It was the middle of the day and these people were not trying to hide anything.

I left my truck with the intention of warning them provided they were co-operative and would not continue to fish. All was fine as I approached them. The roar of the river covered my noise so I was very close before they saw me. One of the men immediately began yelling obscenities and generally flipping out. I kept my distance from the river's edge as the rocks were slippery and a fall into the river could turn this into a very bad day.

I was eventually able to talk the guy down to earth and I told him I would be giving him a warning for fishing in a closed time. I intended to seize his net but I would tell him that at the truck after he'd helped me carry the fish and net back. I was learning.

I put the fish in my truck and he was lifting the net into his truck when I advised him the net was being seized and would be returned when the river opened again. He launched off the ground again and even though I'd introduced myself to him he was calling me all sorts of other names, names that I have never seen in my family tree.

I pulled the net from his hands and put it in my truck. I opened my notebook to write down his vehicle description and licence number and he jumped into his truck, still cursing. I was standing on the side of the road about fifteen feet in front of his truck. He started the motor, glaring at me like a crazed animal, put the truck in gear and punched the gas pedal. The tires were squealing and so was I as I dove toward the ditch just as the front bumper of the truck clipped me on the left knee. I rolled into the ditch in a cloud of dust, still alive but with a sore knee. I dusted off my notebook and started writing a whole lot more.

The fisherman was charged for assault and obstruction, and the eventual trial took place about a year later, but in the course of that year our Crown prosecutor changed after the federal election. This change meant the prosecutor we'd taken so long to train was now the defence lawyer and we had a new and inexperienced lawyer.

I went to court prepared, and presented all the facts and statement. The judge seemed to understand the case and I felt confident. The defence lawyer stood up and advised the courts that the fishery officer identification card I'd produced did not refer to the section of the *Fisheries Act* under which a fishery officer appointment was made. The judge agreed and I left the courtroom dejected. No appeal was filed and new identification cards were issued to the 700 fishery officers in Canada.

Part of the job that was difficult to comprehend was the massive wasting of fish by some people. The Terrace area was especially bad for this in the 1980s. Many jet boat patrols along the river resulted in finding abandoned gillnets full of dead salmon. It was not uncommon to find a gillnet with 100 fish left to rot.

No one can say for certain to whom the nets belonged. The small number of greedy people who tried to make a living selling fish illegally most probably used the abandoned nets. Some nets would break loose from shore and be washed away, catching fish until they were recovered or became entangled on the beach. Regardless of how they came to be, it is certain that thousands of fish were wasted throughout a typical summer. It was always a disappointing sight, not to mention extremely smelly. We found the best way to clean a net was to tie it behind our jet boat and travel full speed until the rotting fish were cleared from the net.

The grim task of pulling abandoned gillnets full of rotting salmon was never fun. The smell on your hands would last for days.

Adventures on Lakelse River

The Lakelse River is about twelve miles long and located near Terrace, flowing from Lakelse Lake to the Skeena River. It's an amazingly productive river, supporting most species of salmon and some trout. Frequently used by recreation anglers and canoeists, it was included along many of our patrols.

Pink salmon were prolific every two years on the Lakelse River with over a million pinks in some years. This would attract many of the less law-abiding fishermen who'd claim to be fishing for other legal species.

On one such patrol I took a remote road down to the river, and on the way in I met a truck coming out. There wasn't room to pass each other so it was easy to stop the truck. The two men in it acted very suspiciously. They had fishing rods and reels in the pickup box but no fish, claiming they'd been trout fishing but hadn't caught any. I saw a small tree branch in the pickup box that looked as if it had blood on it. I didn't say anything about the stick but asked them if I could search their truck and they agreed.

I looked everywhere I could think of—under the seat of the truck, in the glovebox, under the hood, in the fenders, even under the bumper. The more I searched the less nervous they seemed to get. I thought they had stashed their fish in the bush and might be making a drive out to see if I was around.

I was leaning on the box of their truck, staring at the rods and the branch with blood on it, and I was just about to let them go when I saw the spare tire lying in the box. I leapt up into the box and looked in the centre hole of the rim. A black piece of cardboard was visible. "That's a strange thing," I thought.

I lifted the tire up and five pink salmon fell out. Both men's jaws also fell. They were both charged and had to appear in court where the judge fined them each $500 and forfeited their rods and fish.

German tourists also frequent the Terrace area for fishing and hunting, and Lakelse River seemed to attract them. On a sunny day during the pink run I happened across two of them standing on a bridge over the river. One had a video camera and was filming the salmon below. I talked to them briefly before checking a few fishermen upstream of the bridge.

When I approached two anglers to check their gear and licences, one of them asked why I had let the tourists go. I asked what he meant. He said they'd caught at least four pink salmon and had even filmed some of it. I finished my check and hurried back to the bridge just as the two tourists were making their way to their camper. All at once their understanding of English disappeared.

Over the next half hour I was able to find their fishing rods and eight pink salmon hidden in their camper. I was just about finished when I told them I was taking their video camera and film. I told them I'd return the camera the next day. The film did indeed contain footage of them catching salmon and several of the fish in the video were foul hooked. Some were left on the bank for a while before being returned to the water. The quality of their film even impressed the judge, who gave them both a large fine and forfeited their rods. Outside the courtroom they told me they weren't coming back to Canada. Why do people think I should be unhappy about that?

A third Lakelse fishing story involved another lawbreaker who definitely knew better. Some of the fishing holes were very remote and only accessible by walking. I left my vehicle one day to check a number of these sites. I'd walked about half a mile and checked a couple of fishing spots with no one present. The third one had a single male fisherman. I watched from a hidden vantage point about twenty-five yards from him. He was retrieving his line with a fast jerking or jigging motion. I'd seen enough for evidence before I approached him.

He turned and looked at me and then he looked at his fishing rod. He took the cigarette from his mouth and touched it to the fishing line. The line fell slack and the current carried it away. I'd been had by a very old fishing trick. I needed the hook on the line to prove he was fishing. I wasn't a happy guy. I took his fishing rod and asked him to wait for me. He just smiled and said he could wait.

I returned to my truck for my chest waders and walked back to the spot. The fisherman watched with curiosity as I put on my waders and stepped into the river. I slowly walked across the river looking down into the water. I was trying to catch the fishing line by wading back and forth downstream of where he'd cut his line. My efforts seemed futile even to me but I don't like to lose. The water was near the top of my waders a few times but I kept at it for about half an hour before I saw some fishing line across the boot of my waders. I lifted my foot and pulled the line in. A large treble hook was attached and the end of the line appeared to be burned off.

Any lawyer reading this would say, "So what? You can't prove that's his." The same thought went through my mind. I went back to the beach to talk to the fisherman but I never even had to ask. He just blurted out, "That was amazing. I can't believe you just found my line by wading in the water. I'm impressed!" After I'd given him some paperwork he was not as impressed.

Pipelines and Corporate Arrogance

A major natural gas company contracted a company to install a distribution line in the Terrace area in 1981. The pipeline installation had had some delays and had missed the timing window that would allow in-stream crossings but the company was now trying to cut corners and cross streams without applying for permission. One day I was shocked to find a large excavator right in the middle of Williams Creek, near Terrace, digging a channel through an area where sockeye salmon had spawned a few weeks earlier.

I immediately stopped the operation, to the dismay of the crew. The foreman soon learned I was not in a good mood. I advised him that all the equipment on site could be seized for destruction of fish and fish habitat. That seemed to get his attention and improve his co-operation. I took a few statements from crew members and learned the company was aware of the restrictions on the creek but had decided to proceed regardless. This was a trait I would often encounter in the future with large corporations and it caused me to coin the term "corporate arrogance."

Corporate greed and the push for profit will often trump concerns for the environment. Today most companies understand the public's awareness of the environment and will spend millions to convince the public they are good environmental stewards. Any time a large company initiates an ad campaign, you can almost be certain they have recently been caught on the wrong side of the law or are trying to avert a bad reputation. Companies that take their environmental responsibilities seriously rarely need to advertise.

Meanwhile, back in Williams Creek I knew I needed an important piece of evidence. I had to search the mounds of gravel piled by the creek and find salmon eggs. It's much like looking for a needle in a haystack. The eggs are often crushed or float away when displaced. I searched for over an hour by digging with my bare hands but at last I found one live salmon egg and one dead salmon egg. (Dead salmon eggs appear white.) This became a crucial piece of evidence.

I left the site with my evidence and headed back to the office. All the information was put together and the company was charged. They hired a high-priced lawyer to convince the judge of their innocence but they were convicted of destroying fish and fish habitat and fined $5,000. Their construction had to wait until spring, when the salmon eggs had hatched and left the stream.

Enforcement of environmental laws is vital for the future of salmon and all fish species but many large corporations and companies operating in western Canada have a different view. Fishery officers doing their job of protecting fish habitat in Alberta and Saskatchewan didn't get high approval ratings from some prairie folk. Whether it was the result of successful lobbying or the government's changed priority on fish habitat, or a mere coincidence, the number of fishery officers in the Prairie Region was reduced from about fifty-five to fifteen in 2013. While some may claim there are fewer violations in the prairies (well, there would be with fewer officers), others believe the government is moving away from fish habitat protection in this area. Whatever the reason, the fish are the losers.

Pipelines and other forms of linear development (power lines, roads, railroads, etc.) can take place with minimal impact, but taking away the few staff able to monitor this development reminds me of words written by the Honourable John Fraser (former minister of fisheries and author of the report *Fraser River Sockeye 1994: Problems & Discrepancies*). He stated that to say that we cannot conduct enforcement due to budget restraints is "an abdication of the government's constitutional responsibility."

Nature's Waterslide

Mike, a seasonal fishery officer, and I had flown into the gorgeous Gitnadoix valley to count spawning sockeye and the pilot had made a smooth landing on the lake near the mouth of the creek that we had to walk.

Mike and I slipped on our chest waders and started walking up the creek counting sockeye as we went. It was a good return for the creek this year. We rounded a curve in the river just as a lone wolf waded out in the stream about thirty yards in front of us. We both froze and watched in awe. The wolf was unaware of our presence and focused his attention on the salmon swimming around his feet.

The wolf surveyed the fish much like someone deciding which watermelon to buy in the grocery store. He picked out one he liked, lunged for it and waded across the rest of the creek before disappearing into the heavy brush on the bank. We looked at each other in disbelief at what we'd just witnessed before continuing upstream. I couldn't help but feel sorry for the poor sockeye that had battled incredible odds to return to his natal stream only to be plucked from his marital bed in the throes of passion.

In an hour we reached the falls that feed the creek. We'd covered the distance fairly quickly and decided we'd check the

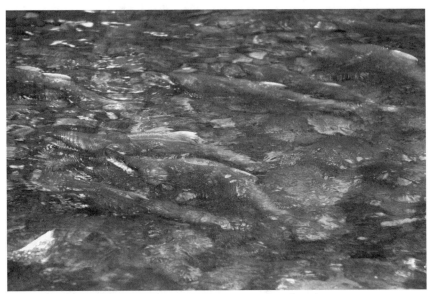

Until the early 1990s, fishery officers walked many miles of remote streams each fall, counting spawning salmon.

falls out. We worked our way through the heavy timber paralleling the falls, which were steep at the bottom but sloped off near the top. The rocks were worn smooth across the width of the falls and sloped down at about a forty-five-degree angle, much like a rooftop.

I'll never know why I did it but I took a step onto the edge of the falls. The slimy surface of the rocks caused me to fall forward and the next thing I knew I was sliding on my butt and heading for disaster. There was nothing I could do. It happened so fast and my speed gave me little time to think but I do remember thinking, "I'm going to break a leg and not be able to run."

I covered the fifty feet of slimy rock in a flash before being launched over the edge. I really thought I would die. I knew the drop was very long with nothing but rocks below. I crested the lip of the falls and dropped about ten feet into a small pool of water on a ledge in the middle of the falls. Someone was taking care of me. A few feet on either side and I would have fallen about fifty feet onto rocks.

My waders quickly filled with water as I sat in the pool. At least

I think it was water, because it was cold. I looked around and all I could do was laugh, realizing how very lucky I was.

Poor Mike had witnessed what he certainly felt was the end of me. He made his way down through the trees to try to find me and I'll never forget the look on his face as he peered over the lip of the falls from the trees. He looked as though he'd seen a ghost. He heard me laughing and couldn't believe his eyes. "I thought you were dead," he stammered. "Why did you do that?" he shouted. "I didn't plan on that trip," I blurted out as I pulled myself to my feet and poured some of the water from the top of my waders.

I reached the bank of the falls and dumped the rest of the water out before we made our way back to the waiting Beaver aircraft. I went home that night and told Lorraine about my day. She was getting used to hearing about close calls because I seemed to be having far too many. That night I felt as if someone had beaten me with a two-by-four, so I guess my landing wasn't totally soft.

Tons of Fun

I took a strange call one winter day in the Terrace office. The call was from a local garage that said they were changing oil on two large vans and the hoist wouldn't lift them. One mechanic had looked in one of the vans and had found it was full of fish with a cardboard cover over the window. That was odd!

The drivers of the vans had left for lunch and returned just as I arrived at the garage. They both were obviously nervous to see me. "What's in the vans, guys?" I asked. "Commercially caught fish that we're taking to Edmonton," one replied. That could be legal but I asked if I could see the fish. They obliged and opened the rear doors of the vans.

Both vans were stuffed with frozen halibut and spring salmon, all of them commercially stamped by a fish plant in Prince Rupert. The men couldn't produce any receipts for the fish so I called the fish plant. The fish plant didn't have any record of such a large sale and the people there were very interested to learn about the fish.

One of the drivers worked in the fish plant and it turned out the two men had stolen the fish and were transporting them to Edmonton to sell. The investigation found they'd made several trips to Edmonton selling fish in the past year. The two vans were brand new two-tonners and they contained an incredible 16,000 pounds of fish: 300 spring salmon and 800 halibut. The fish were seized and returned to the fish plant the next day.

The two drivers were charged but not convicted because the fish plant could not provide an accurate record of their inventory to show any loss. The two men claimed to have bought them from a guy on the dock in Prince Rupert named Steve and they didn't know the fish were stolen. They didn't know how to get in touch with him or where he lived. Yeah, right! They told a great fish story. There was nothing else that could be done. The fish were not returned to the men and they mysteriously stopped selling fish in Edmonton. They both had to find new jobs as well.

Burn and Blast

On March 30, 1980, a report came in about a truck tanker oil spill near Lava Lake in the Nass Valley. I called Greg Caw from the Fish and Wildlife Branch to accompany me and check the report. The roads were icy and heavy with snow. An hour later we arrived at the scene.

The truck and both trailers were lying half submerged under the ice in Lava Lake. Fortunately the driver had only minor injuries and had been taken to town. We walked along the shore to survey the wreckage. It was obvious both tankers had been ruptured as the smell of gas and diesel hung heavy in the air. Fuel was visible on the water near the tanker. There wasn't much we could do at the spill site. It was too dangerous to climb down to the truck. A large tow truck had been dispatched to try retrieving the truck and trailer.

Greg and I returned to Terrace. We both contacted fuel spill experts with our agencies to develop a plan and deal with the fuel spill. Unbelievably, the solution that the experts agreed upon was to burn the fuel off. The gasoline would mostly evaporate leaving the diesel and some gas to burn. No one had a good idea how to ignite the spill though.

Two days later the truck and trailers were removed from the

A trucker failed to navigate the icy roads of the Nass Valley but survived the crash as his truck rolled into Lava Lake and spilled thousands of gallons of diesel and gasoline into the lake.

water. Greg and I headed to the spill site not really knowing how we would tackle this. We arrived to see the brown fuel mixture contained within the hole in the ice with some fuel on top of the ice. We thought of a few options to ignite the fuel and then tried our first idea.

I soaked a rag in fuel and lit it. The road was about fifty feet higher than the lake so I heaved the flaming rag at the spill but I didn't quite throw it far enough and the rag burned out. My next idea was a road flare. I took it from my truck and discussed the option with Greg. Neither of us was anxious to go down the bank and ignite the spill so we did the right thing: we flipped a coin. He lost.

I stood on the bank with my camera as Greg carried the burning flare in his hand. He reached the spill's edge without incident. Neither of us was certain when or if it would ignite. Greg slowly reached out with the flare. He did it with the same care that an athlete would take to light the Olympic flame. A small flame started right away and quickly erupted.

Greg scrambled up the bank and I began snapping pictures. Within seconds flames were climbing two or three hundred feet in the air. The roaring sound of the fire was deafening. We stared in awe as the fire burned violently. Nothing gets the testosterone flowing like a humongous roaring fire. It took over an hour before the flames began to subside and several hours before the fire ran out. We should have taken some wieners!

We inspected the shoreline and found only a small amount of black ash and residue from the fire. We returned to Terrace and reported our successful fuel spill cleanup. Fuel spills today are normally responded to with cleanup crews and proper equipment but this certainly worked under the conditions we had.

Dealing with a fuel spill wasn't the only thing done differently over thirty years ago. Another part of the job practised until the mid-1980s was dealing with problem beavers. Beavers are often responsible for damming streams and preventing spawning salmon

Igniting and burning a gasoline/diesel spill can certainly raise the heart rate and the temperature.

from gaining access to gravel upstream. It was standard practice to remove the dams using explosives, allowing fish to ascend the watercourse.

I'd taken the approved blaster's course and was qualified to use dynamite, and George was a very experienced blaster so he and I were often sent to do the job. It might be a man thing, but watching an explosion is always fun. The blasts would fill the sky with mud, rocks, sticks and probably the occasional beaver. The practice is not used today as the blasts are thought to cause damage to existing fish habitat created by the dams. I'm sure the beaver sleep better today knowing George and I won't be showing up with a few sticks of our own.

Budget Cuts Again

B udget cuts are a part of working in government. No political party is above slashing programs that will negatively impact the fisheries resource, and every party is capable of reversing those cuts depending on the mood of the public and how much politicians feel they can push the envelope one way or the other.

My first experience with this downward cycle was in 1980. I also learned that if you sat and were silent nothing would change. I didn't sit very often. A working fishery officer must face the public every day while the politicians must answer to the public — or at least appear to. Strong public support often provides the highest chance of change to protect fish and wildlife resources.

It's very rare that senior managers take the concerned message from the field to Ottawa, partly due to concerns over being employed (or not) and partly because most senior managers come with a science or biology background. They stay in their comfort zone and honestly believe science and management can solve most problems. I agree these are all important but they need the support of a solid enforcement program or the resource cannot continue. A clear example was the launching of the Salmonid Enhancement Program (SEP) in 1977.

I considered "finishing off" my patrol jalopy, held together with wire, duct tape and luck, but driving it was better than walking everywhere.

A senior SEP manager told me (when I had six months' experience) that the SEP program would be so successful we wouldn't need any enforcement. I didn't believe his words but it taught me how some think. As it turned out, I think my foresight was more accurate than his.

In Terrace I drove a dilapidated, unsafe piece of crap for a vehicle when I worked there. I had to speak out about it and I finally wrote a letter to someone several levels above my supervisor. I described the vehicle and included the following excerpts:

> I am also tired of the constant ridicule I am receiving from the public. The vehicle looks as bad as it sounds. The public has accused me of abusing government property. If the present state of the vehicle resulted from my abuse, fine, I would suffer the consequences, but the vehicle was far past maturity when I received it.

> Another recent incident involved taking a load of garbage from the office to the dump. Upon my arrival the Cat operator told me where

to park (pointing to a pile of wrecked vehicles) and offered to give me a ride to town.

The letter received some attention but not enough until I asked an RCMP officer to do a safety inspection of the vehicle. It was condemned and parked the next day. A lease vehicle was obtained until a new one could be ordered. This was a big victory for a lowly front-line employee.

The vehicle replacement was followed by a major budget freeze, meaning I had a working vehicle but couldn't afford to travel anywhere with it. I reminded myself not to get rational or try making sense of it. There are times when common sense is not that common.

New Adventures in New Aiyansh

I successfully competed against seven other officers for a posting in New Aiyansh, about sixty miles north of Terrace on the Nass River, in 1982. In the early 1980s the logging boom was over and the town of Nass Camp was shrinking. The Nass Valley had three Nisga'a villages with a total population of about 3,000 people.

Lorraine and I were keen to try a new area. We were expecting our first child in October. I knew I'd be busy at work because the officer before me was known for only working nine to five and wasn't really interested in enforcement work. I would also be working with my friend Randy Webb, who'd relocated to Stewart a year earlier.

Our government-supplied accommodation was a very old trailer. We were young and eager and our expectations were lower than most, given we were both from rural Saskatchewan, but our enthusiasm was over the first day. We tolerated the unfit trailer until I walked in for lunch to find the baby crying and Lorraine down on her knees with a shoe in her hand pounding a seriously flattened mouse into the floor. The mouse was about the size of a pancake and she didn't stop pounding it until I tapped her on the shoulder and said, "I think it's dead."

There was no humour in that sight at the time. I knew I had to take some action, as no one should be expected to live in such a place. I went straight to the office and wrote a memo about the trailer. The following words are from that memo:

Day 1: While unpacking our belongings on our first day here, I had occasion to use the washroom. Upon flushing the toilet, excrement in various stages of decomposition came gurgling up into the bathtub. The septic field tank was filled and the lines were plugged. This event did not go far in convincing us this would be a nice place to live. The septic tank was located by digging by hand for two days, as a machine was not readily available.

Day 3: Time to wash clothes. The washing machine had several cups of dog food in it, packed in by mice. Mice were everywhere, chewing up any groceries that weren't in sealed containers. We have to wash our dishes before and after we eat. On our third night my wife awoke to a mouse chewing on her hair.

Day 5: Heavy rain resulted in several wet spots in the trailer. The roof must have been leaking for some time, because the living room carpet and chesterfield were rotten. The furniture and carpet were replaced. The chesterfield was too large to get out the door so a chainsaw was used to cut it into pieces.

The washing machine quit and was taken to Terrace for repairs. It was over two months before it was fixed. This was a great inconvenience, especially with clothes for a six-month-old child.

A week after the washer was repaired the furnace quit. It took four service calls from Terrace and over two months to have it fixed. With the furnace repaired, the hot water tank quit. The parts took over a month to arrive.

Two days later the water heater quit again. A new tank took two weeks to arrive. We were a total of two months without hot water.

We have given up trying to control the mice. The porch is dangerously wired with extension cords and has cracks large enough for squirrels to enter. Squirrels chewed up my wife's brand new leather boots and I continue to pay rent for these "outdoor experiences."

When first reading this memo one might doubt such a series of events could plague one individual. If in doubt, phone my wife.

The letter resulted in free rent and a new house being built in a record time of eight months.

The work in the Nass Valley kept me hopping. I found illegal fishermen everywhere I went. Word was getting around the community and some people were resisting and complaining to the chief and council. I had started by warning everyone and giving their gillnets back the first time. However, a few persisted and charges had to be laid.

One afternoon I patrolled Canyon City and was disappointed to find six gillnets set during the closed time. I pulled them and returned to my office. All the fishermen eventually came to the office asking for their nets. Five of them were polite and agreed they wouldn't set their nets in the closed time and were issued warnings.

The sixth guy came to my office and broke into a verbal tantrum. I couldn't get him to calm down and I refused to return his net. He stormed out of the office and spun gravel all over the front of the office and into our daughter's sandbox as he sped away.

I was invited to a town hall meeting in Canyon City later that fall. I expected a lot of heat from the community but knew attending could be an opportunity to discuss my concerns. The meeting was going fairly well until one man stood up and accused me of treating people differently. I didn't recognize him and wasn't exactly sure what he meant. He said I'd seized a bunch of nets and returned them all except one and that person was charged. My mind went blank and I couldn't remember the incident. The meeting carried on and I left.

I walked the suspension bridge across the Nass River to my truck when I froze in my tracks. I remembered the incident. I thought for a few minutes, debating the pros and cons of returning to the meeting. Would they think I had been lying? Would they agree with the fisherman? I knew I had to go back. It was a very long walk back to the town hall.

I entered the back of the room and stood briefly before the chief noticed me and invited me to the front. I said I had remembered something that was important and thought the community should hear. I proceeded to describe the incident the fishermen had referred to. I agreed that I'd treated him differently because he did not show any respect for me or any respect for the closure. I described how he'd yelled at me and spun his tires, spraying gravel all over the front of the office. I then said, "I'd do the same with anyone else who shows such disregard for me and the fishing closure." The room went very quiet. The fishermen didn't respond.

Then a most shocking thing happened. An elder stood up and started to clap. Within fifteen seconds the entire room (except one) was up and clapping. I was so relieved and knew I'd passed the test in that community. I also learned that elders rule.

Several weeks later Chief James Gosnell (now deceased) came to my office. I couldn't remember a chief ever coming to the DFO office and I wasn't certain why he was there. I'd met him at meetings and found him to be a vocal, well-spoken man who often criticized DFO. He said, "My people are telling me you're very firm with them." I paused, not sure where to take this conversation. James then said, "They also tell me you are being very fair. I wanted to come tell you this because I couldn't say this in public." He smiled, shook hands and left.

That was one of the most powerful, and instructive, meetings I'd ever experienced and it was certainly the shortest. I learned that chief and council are elected and must appear to always be with the people. I also learned that honesty and fairness will gain respect over time. I was challenged less after that.

Lorraine and I had two dogs; hers was a sheltie and I had a shepherd/collie cross. Smokey, my dog, looked like a shepherd and had a very vicious-sounding bark. That dog could be taught nearly anything and provided great companionship on patrols.

I often left Smokey at home with Lorraine and our daughter Dana as there were a few people in the valley who didn't appreciate the work I did. I'd been threatened on more than one occasion, including an anonymous death threat by phone one evening at home. After that incident I left Smokey with Lorraine.

People often came to the house asking about a net that I had seized or to talk about fishing. I always felt safe with Smokey there. He would stand by the door when Lorraine opened it. She would then grab him by the collar to signal "show time." He would bark and lunge like a trained police dog. It usually kept the conversations brief. He'd stop barking the second the door was closed.

The RCMP constable borrowed Smokey whenever he had to work a late shift alone. He'd put Smokey in the back of the Suburban and Smokey seemed to know it was show time again. Whenever the constable came driving in the yard Smokey would wag his tail because he knew he'd have a night of fun with the RCMP. He never bit anyone but if something had happened I'm sure he would have. I'd rather have him working with me than an officer.

Court dates in New Aiyansh were always an adventure. Judges travelled in once every couple of months from Terrace and court was usually held in the gymnasium on Main Street. On one very cold December day when court was scheduled, the furnace in the gymnasium had mysteriously quit. The judge cancelled the trials but he still had to call all the cases and reset dates. He decided it was warmer outside in the sun than inside the gym, and he was right. The judge opened the tailgate of his Suburban and set the files out on the tailgate.

The judge had a great sense of humour as he read through the names and dealt with them all. One man who stood before the judge was chewing gum. The judge said that would not normally be allowed in a courtroom but that it probably kept him warm. The judge also indicated it was the first time he'd ever allowed dogs in the courtroom, as several dogs wandered through. One dog even watered the judge's tires and caused the whole courtroom to burst out laughing. It probably belonged to one of the accused.

The Grizzly Bear Attack

August 30, 1982, was another beautiful sunny morning in the Nass Valley. I walked the ten steps from my trailer porch to my cedar twelve-by-fourteen Pan-Abode office nestled in the tall evergreens and I called Randy Webb, friend and fishery officer in Stewart, BC. We arranged to meet at Meziadin Junction and travel north with the intention of walking Oweegee Creek to count spawning chinook salmon. Walking creeks was one of my favourite parts of the job because you got to see the fruits of your labour, trying to protect the salmon en route to their spawning grounds. I gave Lorraine a kiss, hopped in my DFO truck and headed out along the winding, dusty gravel road through to Cranberry Junction. You had to pay attention to the sixteen-foot-wide logging trucks, calling out their locations along the way. Once I had hit the pavement at Cranberry Junction it was about another hour before I met up with Randy. He had the twelve-foot aluminum boat on his truck so I jumped in with him, taking my shotgun and lunch, two essentials for a day in the north along a salmon creek in the late summer. About an hour north of Meziadin Junction we arrived at Oweegee Lake, unloaded the boat and gear and prepared for the half-hour row across the lake.

I locked the vehicle and was a few yards from the truck when I stopped in my tracks. To this day I don't know why. "I'm going to take my shotgun too today," I said. Randy looked at me rather puzzled because we usually carried one shotgun between the two of us. Both of us had walked many streams and encountered numerous bears without a serious incident. I trusted him and I had my sidearm but I turned and walked back to the truck to get my twelve-gauge shotgun and an extra box of SSG and slugs, something else I'd never done before. I'm sure Randy wondered why I did this but he didn't say anything. We pushed off onto the placid lake and Randy did all the rowing as I'd not mastered the art of rowing backwards. He did a great job and quickly ferried us across the lake. We hauled the boat out, pulled our chest waders on, put our packs on, grabbed the shotguns and started walking down the creek. Neither of us had ever walked this creek before but it quickly became very evident this was serious bear country. The creek was a small tributary about five to seven yards wide with heavy alder growth hanging over both banks. Many areas became very narrow and we constantly had to duck under overhanging limbs and climb over windfalls in the creek. The chinook were spawning and we clicked our "tally-whackers" (hand-held counters) as we made our way through the jungle. More bear tracks! We both discussed the tracks and decided they were far too fresh but never once thought of turning back. This was important work we were doing and the biologists needed to know the spawning numbers. After about half a mile of walking and counting fish Randy climbed over a very large windfall, a tree about a yard off the ground. He'd just climbed over the tree and I was stepping forward to climb over when Randy suddenly yelled, "Get out of here you bastard!"

I had no idea what he meant and later he said he had no idea why he said it either. Whether he had heard something or it was just a premonition we'll never know, but it put us both on high alert. There was nothing visible around us except bushes and creek, and I was just about to ask him why he'd said that when no more than twenty-five feet in front of him the bushes exploded. It was

Grizzly bear encounters were frequent when we walked remote streams in northern BC.

a sow grizzly bear coming directly at him at full speed. Grizzlies can travel at over thirty miles an hour. If you do the math you'll see it doesn't take long for them to cover twenty-five feet. This takes longer to describe than it did to happen. In seconds the bear was virtually on Randy, who somehow managed to jump over the yard-high log with his back toward it. That doesn't seem physically possible, but he cleared the log with ease and landed several feet to my right in the creek. Perhaps that's how Dick Fosbury was inspired to try high jumping backwards!

With Randy no longer in my line of fire I instinctively levelled my shotgun from the hip and fired. I pumped the gun, raised it to my shoulder and took another shot at the bear as it came over the log. I don't remember even thinking about shooting and I wouldn't have had time to think. After the second shot the bear reared up on its hind legs, spun around and ran about twenty yards before dropping by the creek. I looked at Randy and realized he'd fallen when he landed and was sitting in the creek, pasty white. I looked back toward the bear and saw two cubs coming toward us snapping and snarling. I know there will be critics out there who ask why we would shoot the cubs but at that point anything moving was not safe. I yelled at Randy to shoot, as I knew I only had two rounds left.

It was then I realized he'd dropped his shotgun in the creek. He picked it up, poured the water out the barrel, levelled the gun and shot one of the cubs. He fired at the second one but the shot wasn't fatal and the cub made a crying noise that would disturb anyone. I aimed and fired my third round, killing the third bear. We looked at each other for a moment in silence and then Randy started walking in small circles saying, "F#&%! You got those shots off fast." He must have repeated this about five times as he walked around in an obvious state of shock. He said he remembered looking up and seeing the bear coming down on him, smelling the sow's breath and hearing the shots but nothing in between.

I wondered if there might be other bears and remembered my extra rounds, so I took the box from my pocket, opened it and dropped all five rounds on the gravel. My hands were shaking so badly I couldn't load the gun standing up and I had to kneel down and turn the shotgun upside down to slide a couple of rounds in using both thumbs. When I stood up Randy was still walking in circles. I looked down at my right foot and started to laugh. "Look at this Randy!" I said, pointing to my right foot. I had my weight on my left foot and my right foot was moving from side to side in a throbbing motion. I had no control over it. It was an absolutely bizarre feeling. Randy started to laugh too. The adrenaline racing through my veins was causing the involuntary movement. Remarkably, that was the only involuntary movement I had!

After a couple of minutes reality started setting in. We were both concerned that we'd just killed three grizzly bears. What would the conservation officers say? What would the public think? We had no way of contacting anyone. This was before cell phones and radios. I said, "Maybe we should skin them out and take the hides back. Someone might be able to use them." Randy agreed but he had the only knife, a three-inch Swiss Army Knife, and it was very dull. I agreed to try using it, so he sharpened it on a round river rock and we walked toward the dead bears. They were all obviously dead but I don't think either one of us really wanted to touch them. I remember forcing myself to give the sow a poke with the barrel of my gun and jumping back. Nothing happened. I kept the gun in one hand and slowly reached my shaking hand out to touch the bear. Again nothing happened. I asked Randy to keep his gun at hand while I turned the bear over.

I finished skinning the sow and did a fairly good job, or so I thought. The flies were incredible but their bites never registered until the next day. I then skinned one of the cubs, which went more smoothly. We decided to leave the second small bear because it had a gaping hole through the middle. We packed the hides up and then I washed my hands off in the creek. I was having trouble getting the blood off and kept washing and washing until I realized I'd cut myself twice. Despite being large enough to cause concern, the cuts didn't hurt until several hours later. The adrenaline was blocking the pain. We made our way back to the boat, crossed the lake, loaded our truck and headed home. Randy dropped me off at my truck and I made my way back to Nass Camp by about 6 p.m. Lorraine greeted me at the door and I told her a very short version of our day. She asked, "Why'd you shoot the cubs?" That's probably a predictable response from an expectant mother. I fought the urge to say anything and chose to leave this for a later discussion.

I knew my thinking was not very clear yet so I did the best thing I know to clear my head: I went for a ten-mile run. I started my stopwatch and headed out at a very leisurely pace. The run was just what I needed. I looked at my watch. What? Fifty-five minutes! I'd run that fast on pavement but this run felt relaxing and it was on gravel. Again I realized the adrenaline was still in my veins. The next day my muscles were more sore than they should have been. Maybe there should be a caged grizzly bear at the starting line in the Olympics. I think we'd see some new world records.

I told the whole story to Lorraine that evening and she was much more understanding about the bears. I decided to stay up and watch some TV, as I didn't feel tired. I watched TV all night until Lorraine awoke in the morning. I had breakfast and went to work and never felt tired at all. This went on for three days and I never slept a wink. The fourth night I crashed and slept well after that. The bear story spread throughout the community and the department. It seemed everywhere Randy and I went people wanted to hear about it. I still tell the story and every time I do I feel my pulse quicken.

Canyon City Confrontation

On August 31, 1982, I went into the office having not slept a wink from the bear attack the day before. Staying home didn't make sense because I'd just think about it anyway. Besides, being in the mouse-infested trailer called home twenty feet from my office was hardly getting away. Today was a helicopter flight to count salmon in a series of creeks in the Nass Valley. This made a lot more sense to me: no need to worry about bears. (The cost of helicopter flights prevented us from flying many remote streams, which is why we walked them.)

I met the helicopter at noon in Nass Camp where Doug, a seasonal officer, and I discussed our flight plans with the pilot. Then we were gone for three hours, counting 400 spring salmon in the Cranberry River, 25 in the North Seaskinish, 50 in the Tseax and 50 in the Ishkinish, along with about 2,000 pinks. On our return flight to Nass Camp we flew low over the Nass River and as we went over the village of Canyon City we saw several gillnets set on the village side of the river. The river was closed to fishing. We didn't land because we wouldn't have any place to put the nets if we seized them so we returned to Nass Camp and then drove the twenty minutes to Canyon City.

At that time Canyon City was only accessible by a narrow foot suspension bridge about fifty feet above a very fast flowing section of the Nass River. Doug and I parked our vehicle and made our way across the bridge. Our first priority was to get the nets out of the water and then try finding the nets' owners. I'd made numerous efforts to advise them the river was closed and that I had every intention of charging them. Doug and I crawled down the steep rocky bank to the precarious edge where the nets were tied to the shore. We had difficulty pulling the first net from the fast current and removing the fish from the net. We released those that were alive and kept the dead ones. This was a dangerous place to be but it was about to get worse.

Suddenly I saw a fist-sized rock go whizzing by Doug's head and splash in the river. Then another. Then one narrowly missed my head. A larger, head-sized boulder came tumbling down the bank. I quickly realized this was not a natural event and I looked up the bank to see five people standing and yelling at us. On a normal day I would have been terrified of the situation. If any one of those rocks had hit either of us and we had ended up in the river this story would have turned into an inquest. I clearly remember thinking,

Helicopters are costly and used sparingly to patrol remote areas of BC and the Yukon.

"What are these idiots doing? Don't they realize I was attacked by a grizzly bear yesterday? Are they trying to scare me? They are in trouble!" This was hardly clear thinking, but this was happening about twenty-four hours after the bear attack.

I scrambled up the rocks like a proud mountain goat. I went to the group and got right in their space. Again, not clear thinking but it worked. I yelled at them, called them all sorts of unintelligent things and they backed up. I kept moving toward them. I had absolutely no fear. I kept thinking about the bears. These guys were nothing. It was likely that this peculiar approach caught the group off guard. A couple looked at each other, turned and walked back to the village. I'm not even sure of everything I said that day but I did manage to get one to admit and claim his net. I issued him an appearance notice. Once the last one had left Doug and I finished our job and pulled the other two nets and fish and returned to our office. This event probably helped me survive the three years I spent in the Nass as I'm sure the group told the story about the new guy who is just a bit unstable. Someday I'd like to talk to that group and hear the story from their side.

The Terrible Truck Trip to Town

It had been quite the start to a week. I'd had the grizzly bear attack and the Canyon City incident, and it was only Wednesday. Things would get better; I always like to think that. Lorraine and I headed to town for an overnight trip to pick up some building supplies. Doug and I were building a roof over our leaky, rodent-infested trailer. I thought at least we and the mice would be dry. We did some shopping in the afternoon and the evening was spent at the Skeena Valley Marathoners running club meeting. "See, this week is getting better," I thought.

The next day we had a few personal things to deal with like renewing a mortgage at fourteen percent, picking up phones and arranging for a repairman to come fix our washing machine. After our personal work was done we went to Budget Rental to pick up a five-ton truck to haul the building supplies. Time was becoming a factor because Lorraine had an appointment with the nurse practitioner in New Aiyansh that evening. We went to Omineca Lumber and the staff helped us load the truck in record time. The truck was now fully loaded but we managed to squeeze a large quantity of groceries in at the back of the load. The precious flat of eggs was placed on the seat in the cab so they wouldn't be scrambled on the trip home.

Pothole? What pothole? Until it was paved in the 1990s, the gravel logging road to the Nass Valley was famous for close encounters and flat tires.

We headed up the narrow dusty road after a successful day. We were making good time and the pressure of missing a prenatal class had vanished—until the truck started making more noise. A few miles later the muffler dropped and was dragging on the ground. I managed to pull over and stop before it fell off. I crawled under the truck to find it still hanging on at the front. "I can fix this!" I thought. I usually carry haywire and decided to wire it back in place. "Ouch!" It was hot. Ouch again! The mangled muffler was also sharp and I cut my hand. After reciting a few religious words and jumping around from the stinging pain of the burn and the cut I calmed down and Lorraine managed to tie a rag around my hand to stop the bleeding. Back under the truck to tie up the muffler and we were on our way again. Fifteen minutes later I noticed a pickup coming up behind me flashing his headlights. I pulled over to let him pass but he stopped, rolled down his window and said, "Your back door is open and stuff is falling out." I looked back down the road at a trail of juice cartons as far as I could see. I thanked him for letting me know. Looking in the back of the truck I realized we'd lost a couple of cases of juice, another bag of groceries, some shotgun shells and a bag with my running gear in it.

I turned the truck around and we gathered up what was left of the juice cartons, many of which had burst on impact. I met a couple of vehicles that had obviously picked up some of the free groceries on the road. Trying to remain positive, I thought, "Well at least we have our eggs and we can still make the prenatal class. Also, a nurse gives the prenatal class and she can take care of my injuries." I turned the truck around again but now we were tight for time. I pushed the truck fairly hard and made the turn into New Aiyansh thinking we were only a few minutes late. Then, bang! Another big pothole! As if in slow motion, the flat of eggs flew up in the air, turned upside down and landed on the floor between us. Lorraine and I looked at each other and were actually able to laugh at the yolk between us. I didn't stop until we pulled into the nursing station for our class. I stepped out of the truck and the nurse was laughing. I looked around and realized she was laughing at me. I had dust and rust on my face, my back and clothes, a cloth bandage on my finger and egg on my shoes. We proceeded to tell her our story. This was proving to be quite a week.

Dirty Rotten Ice Hole

My working relationship in the Canyon City and New Aiyansh villages had improved, but Greenville was still not receptive to my efforts. Greenville was the most remote community, being located near the mouth of the Nass River and only accessible by boat in the summer.

People would travel across on foot once the river was frozen but the ice was never stable due to tidal influence in the area and more than one person had fallen through and drowned. Today a large bridge provides access but back then walking on broken ice was the only way across in winter.

I was invited to a meeting in Greenville one winter. The organizers told me to wait on the shore and someone would meet me to cross the ice. I travelled with another DFO staff member who would answer any biology-related questions.

We arrived at the parking lot to find a couple of guys waiting for us. One man told us to follow the snowmobiler across the ice so he could show us where to go. The snowmobiler began driving slowly across the ice, meandering around to find where he thought the ice would be the safest. Some areas of open water were visible and made it very unnerving. The biologist went ahead and I followed him.

We were about halfway across when the biologist's left foot broke through the ice. He scrambled out and was wet to his knee. The snowmobiler kept travelling and we thought we'd better keep going. We made the trip across without falling through again.

We arrived at the meeting hall to find a large group. I approached a man I had met and knew and described our crossing to him. He was surprised and asked what route we'd taken. I told him and he asked me to step outside. I was curious why he wanted to speak outside until I heard what he had to say.

He said, "Randy, no one goes around that large rock in the river—that's the thinnest ice on the crossing. Someone wanted you to go in." My heart was in my throat. A thousand images flashed through my mind, including those of my wife and newborn child. I became very angry.

He told me a snowmobile can travel over much thinner ice than a person on foot and the driver had led us to an unsafe area. He told me he couldn't tell anyone else but he wanted me to know. I thanked him sincerely and returned to the meeting.

I sat and listened as the first part of the meeting was for the biologist. I couldn't focus on anything except the apparent attempt that had just been made to drown us. Then my name was called to address enforcement issues to the group. I slowly walked forward and stood at the front of the room. I had to unload.

"Our trip across the ice was a near disaster. My partner got wet up to his knee. I know that some people here would have liked to see me fall through and drown. [The room fell silent.] The route we were led across the river is where people have drowned and everyone here knows that. I will not meet with the people in this room when I know someone here wanted me to die. This meeting is over and I'd like someone to walk in front of us as we return to our truck. I will never come across the ice to this village again."

I left the room unsure where this would go but I wasn't taking it lightly. Two people led the biologist and me back across the river.

We followed them closely and walked lightly. This was a time when I was glad not to be overweight and happy to have size thirteen feet.

There never was any fallout from the meeting. I wasn't asked to another meeting in the winter and the community's compliance improved. It was another very close call. I didn't share the incident with Lorraine for quite a while as I felt she had enough to deal with already.

Logging in the Nass

N ass River logging was a vital economic driver in the valley for many years. I arrived near the end of the "gravy" years. I have observed that companies usually have a way of harvesting the most profitable timber first and then trying to continue to operate with the expectation of the same profits.

I was very fortunate to have worked with George and John in Terrace to learn about the logging industry. Trees were always the largest near streams and companies were constantly pushing the limits to log along watercourses. Stream crossings were constructed with stringers from the largest spruce trees they could find.

In the early 1980s most of these large trees had been taken. Ironically, high pulp prices resulted in the largest spruce trees being logged for pulp, and this contributed to the shortage of bridge stringers and timber in later years. The total lack of planning for such a basic need seemed almost unbelievable to me. Of course I was the bad guy who was stopping their logging by not allowing them to take trees adjacent to the stream.

I found it pathetic how representatives from gigantic companies could plead like starving dogs to get approval for logging near streams. The provincial forestry representatives were not very different. They were pressured by provincial politics to approve logging wherever the companies wanted to go. DFO was really the only watchdog to care for the environment in many northern communities. Sadly, that function is being lost today with changes to the *Fisheries Act* and cuts to budgets.

A new market for cottonwood trees occurred one winter. A company had secured a large contract to provide cottonwood to China and the push was on to find suitable timber to fill the contract. Apparently no one had had the foresight to consider where he or she might find such quantities without impacting fish habitat.

Cottonwood only grows in wet areas, usually in ideal coho fry habitat. Many a discussion took place with companies and again I was the mean guy stopping them from logging. They became so desperate that a couple took chances and logged in areas without seeking approval.

I showed up in the middle of one such site and stopped the logging. If they had approached us prior to logging, we could have reached a solution and allowed logging of a large portion of the area, but they chose to clear-cut the entire area, filling in coho habitat with limbs, snow and debris.

When companies are caught, their first words are often, "We can clean this up." In some cases they could, even if it meant removing material by hand, but it was often a losing battle as pressure to fulfill the contract rose.

The local First Nations were in on some of the logging too. A large island in the Nass River at the mouth of the Tseax River was clear-cut without authorization. The loss of trees caused the island to erode away the following year along with the total loss of fish habitat. I was directed not to proceed with an investigation and was never given a reason.

I found most loggers and truck drivers to be responsible, concerned citizens. It was the companies pushing them, putting them under pressure to take shortcuts, that caused problems. I fully understood that logging and development had to take place. I also knew it could be done with minimal impact on profits if everyone was reasonable, but too often companies take the path of least resistance, sometimes through politicians.

Logging requires roads, often built to a lower standard, and the dusty roads and sixteen-foot-wide logging trucks always presented a challenge in the Nass Valley. They were allowed to be that size because this was an industrial logging road. It's intimidating to see one barrelling down the road at you.

The truckers were very reliable at using radio calls to announce their location. Our vehicles were equipped with radios and we did the same. Things were safe as long as everyone used the radio. Trucks normally only hauled on weekdays, but the radios were always used just in case someone was on the road on a weekend.

I was travelling down the road along the Nass River through a narrow, winding section one day when I came around a corner to see a huge truck pulling a low-bed trailer loaded with a very large excavator and nowhere to go. There wasn't time to brake or even think. If I ran into the grille of this loaded train of iron it would be over. I cranked the steering wheel to the right and drove into the ditch.

The rocks and stumps jolted me to a sudden stop as the cloud of dust from the loaded truck went screaming by my window. "I'm still in one piece," I thought. I climbed out the door and stepped onto the road just as the driver of the truck came running up to me. "I'm so sorry," he said. "I didn't call on the radio. Are you okay?"

I was a little dazed but relieved that he'd stopped and admitted his mistake. He helped pull my vehicle back onto the road with his truck. The steering was a bit distorted, but I managed to drive home. Another lucky day!

Incidentally, Nass Camp had a Logger's Sports Day that Lorraine and I attended. The events included obstacle bucking (with a chainsaw), axe throw, two-man crosscut, log stacking and choker setting. A friend talked me into entering even though I'd never set a choker.

My fitness level made up for my lack of skill and I won the event. I was declared the "Bull of the Woods" and received the overall trophy. That was funny!

Using My Psychic Powers

First Nations fishers were not restricted to an individual quota. They were allowed to catch what they needed. Each band or nation was limited to a catch ceiling. The difficulty arose from not knowing exactly how many fish were caught, and part of a fishery officer's job was to gather catch information. That sounds fairly simple except that very few fishermen were interested in passing the correct catch figures on. (This is no different from commercial or sport fishers.)

I tried to check as many nets and boats on the river as possible and calculate the total through extrapolation. I found I could not rely on catch figures given to me verbally without having some way to validate them. I needed a plan. Most of the fishing boats came into one key landing on the river. I spent many hours waiting for boats to arrive but I couldn't be there all the time. I focused my plan on the main landing.

I was waiting for boats to come in one day and started looking around the bank of the river. I found a very large cottonwood tree with a hole on the backside. I peered in the opening and found the tree was hollow, as the centre had rotted away. It was a tight fit but I found I could squeeze into the tree, as long as a bear wasn't in there first.

On my next trip to the landing I carried a knife and a saw. I climbed inside the tree and proceeded to carve a small hole through the front of the tree. The opening allowed me to view the landing area and I could see down into any boat that came in. My plan was complete.

I didn't drive my vehicle down to the site the next day; I ran the three miles from my office. No one was at the landing but a number of boat trailers were parked there so I knew people were out fishing. I climbed into the tree and waited.

The boats came in and I was able to count the fish accurately. I did this for a number of days and made a note of how many each person had brought in.

The final part of the plan was to approach some of the fishermen in the village while they were talking to other fishermen. I would strike up a conversation and ask how they'd done fishing the day before. They'd usually act surprised that I knew they'd been out. I asked them how many fish they'd caught. I was always given a low number. I would then correct them in front of their friends, telling them all exactly how many fish and what species they'd caught. The shocked look on their faces was priceless.

I continued this practice for a couple of weeks. I suggested they should do a better job of providing accurate catch numbers because I had ways of finding out.

Rumours came back to me that I must have some psychic powers because I was able to tell them how many fish they'd caught. Fishermen started providing more accurate numbers after that. The accuracy of catch data improved and no one ever found out—unless someone from the Nass Valley reads this story today.

Flying Fish

I 'd received reports of a certain fisherman from the Hazelton area coming up to the Meziadin area to catch fish. He was allowed to fish in the area but he was taking large numbers and selling them.

One evening I made the ninety-minute drive to check the Meziadin. Just as I was approaching the fishing site a vehicle was coming out. I recognized the driver as the person I was looking for. He stopped and got out of his truck. I didn't remember him being so large. So very large.

The man admitted he'd been fishing and walked to the back of his pickup to lift the lid on the large wooden box for my inspection. The box was stuffed with 200 sockeye; most were in overfilled burlap bags but some lay loose on top of them. Upon initial inspection they appeared to be legally marked (years ago, First Nations were required to mark their fish by cutting the noses and dorsal fins off their fish to prevent them from entering the commercial market).

I climbed into the truck box as the fisherman stood with his arms folded. I rolled up my sleeves and reached down through a slimy bag to grab a fish from down deep. I pulled the fish out to find it wasn't marked. I reached in again and repeated this with all the bags. The fisherman was getting angry because his plan hadn't worked.

He appeared even larger now than when he'd exited the truck. I knew I could run faster than him and wasn't too concerned about a fight, but then he reached over the side of the truck and started flinging the 80- to 100-pound sacks of fish through the air like pillows. The bags would hit the road and explode, tossing sockeye in every direction. He was yelling and cussing and didn't stop until the box was empty. Actually, he missed one bag. I thought about telling him but didn't want to send him off on another rant.

I talked for quite a while before I thought it was safe to step out of the truck and begin dealing with him. He eventually calmed down. I will always remember the flying fish and how effortlessly he tossed those sacks of sockeye.

Operation Roundup

DFO conducted a major undercover operation that started in the summer of 1982. Two retired undercover RCMP officers were hired for four months to set up a fish-buying business. Their goal was to purchase fish illegally in the Lower Mainland and target buyers who were purchasing the fish as well. The undercover team purchased fifteen tons in one day from one location and over sixty tons in three months, mostly from First Nations. The illegal sale of salmon was widespread and out of control.

I was called to Vancouver on January 11, 1983, for "Operation Roundup." The coordinated dawn raid took place early the following day when forty vehicles were seized and the majority of people served with appearance notices. The operation resulted in about 100 people being charged. Only one incident turned ugly and that was when a fisherman tried to break into a tow truck.

Although the operation identified the problem, success in court was very limited and the political fallout was more than Ottawa could sustain. It was DFO's largest ever "catch and release program"—most of the charges were negotiated away.

Illegal sales persist in many areas today. There may not be a solution until commercial companies stop buying the fish. To properly deal with illegal sales would require increased resources that no government seems willing to provide. Some court rulings have also directed government to move to some form of legal sales and others have ruled sales were unlawful, further complicating enforcement.

Some bands have dealt with illegal sales by working with DFO and penalizing their own members. As in most crime, it's a small number who abuse the law, and the benefits usually support their other criminal activities. Salmon is often another form of criminal currency.

Some bands have negotiated sales agreements with DFO and others have started "pilot sales." These changes are inevitable; however, they further complicate an already difficult enforcement task. People buying fish must be especially diligent to ensure they are purchasing legal product and to avoid the serious health risks associated with improperly handled fish. Tests have shown that a high percentage of fish seized from poachers by fishery officers is unfit for human consumption.

I expect traditional salmon ocean commercial fisheries to continue their slow evolution away from mixed ocean fisheries, moving instead to inland river fisheries that target specific stocks. Ironically, DFO is closing a number of Interior offices and moving officers to coastal areas. I'm sure the next inquiry will correct this mistake. I also believe technological advancements in DNA analysis will someday provide a tool that can instantly analyze a fish scale to determine its natal stream; if the fish is from a weak run it could be tagged and released.

It's high time that First Nations, provincial and federal governments get down to serious land claims settlements, which would provide a more permanent solution. Fish are an important element in these discussions but somehow we have to move forward. The problem is compounded by changing leadership every few years in all camps and by differing views on how to proceed. It's very easy for a government to shelve progress in favour of more realistic, attractive short-term goals to increase the chances of re-election.

Quesnel: Let the Games Begin!

I was successful in a competition for a Quesnel job early in 1985. Lorraine and I were ready for the move. We had made some great friends in the Nass Valley but an isolated place can sneak up on you and we were beginning to be aware of that.

We knew it was time to go when:

- The highlight of the week was mail day.
- I could change a tire in four minutes and ten minutes later do it again. The roads were terrible on tires and we always carried two spares.
- I patched a third flat tire by driving a nail into it and putting glue on it. It worked!
- We started recognizing individual mice and squirrels.
- I didn't like driving on pavement.
- A teacher walking down the road dressed in camouflage and with a rifle over his shoulder was not considered odd (and it wasn't hunting season).
- A second teacher seen wandering around in the dark wearing a housecoat and a smile was okay too.

The Nisga'a people were a pleasure to deal with. Sure, there were a number of horrible incidents with a few of them but the overall support and respect they gave me was a true learning experience. I learned so much about First Nations politics and who really makes the decisions in a community. I will always cherish those three years in the Nass Valley.

So Lorraine and I moved to Quesnel. It was early in the year and I had a few months to become familiar with local poaching sites before the first sockeye arrived. I soon realized there were more poaching sites than I had imagined and the problem was compounded by the fact that virtually everyone in the community was involved in illegal fishing.

Going down to the river at night with a group of friends to catch some "Chilcotin Turkeys" was acceptable to almost everyone—schoolteachers, loggers, social workers, farmers and just about anyone else who wanted to participate. My boss told me there wasn't much I could do about it without a lot of support. I took it as a personal challenge and worked with a seasonal officer, Franz Lorenz, to tackle the problem.

In the first summer we charged over seventy poachers and nearly every one of them tried to run away. We only charged those we'd observed fishing even though they would be in groups of up to a dozen. Over the course of five years the number of poachers decreased and the type of person poaching changed from ordinary local to hardened criminal. During the fifth summer we apprehended twenty-one poachers; every one had a serious criminal record and eighteen of the twenty-one had records with violence.

Running had become an important part of my life. I was getting faster all the time and beginning to realize I could combine my running skill with catching poachers. This was to be a great place to work and these were some of the most enjoyable summers of my life.

As summer approached, work switched over to fishing activities so I did some work with the conservation officers early in the season. We checked a local stream where trout spawned. Poachers sometimes went into the creeks to gaff and net spawning trout.

I was on patrol of Barlow Creek with conservation officer Jim Corbett one day when we saw two young men down by the creek as we drove along a road above it. One had a dip net in his hand. As we rolled to a stop about 100 feet above their location both of the men dropped everything and began sprinting up the far steep bank of the creek.

I jumped out of the truck, sprinted down the near bank and started climbing the far one. They had a good head start and I was loaded down with all my gear and wearing large hiking boots, but I caught the man I'd seen fishing with the dip net before he'd gone 400 yards. He was shocked that I'd caught him but not as shocked as Jim was when I returned to the truck like a proud Labrador retriever. Jim couldn't stop laughing as we dealt with the young man.

The net, trout and packs were seized and he was issued an appearance notice for court. Jim hadn't known that I was a competitive runner until that afternoon. He observed, "The poachers in Quesnel will be very surprised this summer."

A few days later Jim took me to another trout spawning creek. We could see three men by the creek as we approached. They started to run away as I bailed out of the truck like a hound and started the chase. I went after the one I'd seen in the creek with the dip net again. I was a bit disappointed the chase didn't last longer. The poacher was surprised someone had chased him down. He commented, "You're new here, aren't you?" I smiled back, "If you know I'm new then you must do this type of poaching often and I'll get to know you better." It was hard to hide my enthusiasm. I wanted to chase some more.

Placer Miners

I arrived in Quesnel in the spring just as the placer miners started up their operations. They were an eclectic group of individuals indeed. Virtually every one of them had a glazed-over gaze from dreaming about getting rich. The only impediment to their riches was DFO, or so it seemed to me.

The environmental impact of placer mining can be disastrous unless proper guidelines are followed. Following the guidelines meant a moderate amount of additional work, which these "pioneer thinkers"—who felt their placer lease gave them the right to conduct any activity they felt necessary—were unwilling to do.

The provincial mines branch was supportive of the industry and not so concerned about the environment. This became blatantly evident when I caught the local mines inspector giving wrong advice and directions to miners on several occasions.

One of the first violators I encountered was a man who had strong political ties to the provincial government and was directly involved with the BC Mining Association. His cavalier attitude was difficult to alter. He thought he could use his political ties to stop my pursuit of his illegal activities and it took him several days of phoning people to find out I could only be influenced through

Ottawa. Not that DFO was above political influence, but it became difficult for him to use his provincial ties for a DFO violation.

He finally saw the light after charges were laid and he was convicted at trial. His compliance did improve but it gave me a taste of what to expect in the placer industry. There were very few miners who followed the rules and more than one who seemed to have sniffed far too much mercury and other chemicals. One genius miner suggested, "All miners should be allowed to silt up the creeks; that would help flush out the Fraser River."

Some wore side arms while on their claims to "protect themselves." Some were paranoid about others stealing their gold. I felt I was back in the 1800s at times. One miner tried to convince me that the fish in his settling pond resulted from a merganser eating fish eggs in the river and passing the eggs through its intestines, and then the eggs hatched out in his pond. Some reminded me of an older fishery officer's quote, "His toughest four years in school were Grade 2." There may have been some ethical, environmentally minded miners but I never met any of them.

The Polite Poacher

Franz and I were on a nighttime patrol along the Fraser River in early July of my first summer in Quesnel. Franz was a magician at walking the trails at night. Not only did he have an incredible knowledge of the area, but he had remarkable night vision.

We drove to an area known as Kersley, south of Quesnel along the Fraser River. We parked our vehicle well away from the river and began walking down a series of trails in the dark. It was important not to use flashlights or the poachers would be alerted to our approach. We didn't have access to night vision equipment and had to get very close to identify people fishing. If we weren't sure someone was fishing, there wasn't much chance we could charge him or her.

The trail looked as though it had some fresh footprints. We walked very slowly as we approached the open gravel bar of the river and then we stood still to watch and listen. We heard some voices and saw the silhouettes of people standing on the shore about 200 yards upstream from our location. We could see four or five people.

We came up with a plan that we thought would work. Putting Franz's knowledge of trails together with my running abilities, we decided that Franz would circle around upstream of the group while I would sneak in as close as I could get and try identifying who was fishing in the group. We had portable radios and my signal would be two clicks on the radio. Once I signalled Franz he would turn on his flashlight and approach the group from upstream and hopefully get everyone running in my direction.

The large rocks on the riverbank made it very difficult to walk without making noise but I wore running shoes for nights like this as they were quiet on the rocks and easy to run in when the chase was on. I crouched down and placed each foot on a firm rock. Then I would feel around with my hands to find a place to take my next step without spooking the group.

I crossed the open gravel bar with care. It took about twenty minutes to get within twenty yards of the fishing stand. (Cariboo poachers often built a "dip stand" in the river. It was much like a small boardwalk anchored to the shore. They'd stand on the end and use a dip net to scoop fish out of the river.) My heart was pounding and my mouth went dry. I was amazed how close I could get. The trick was not to move quickly and to stand absolutely still if anyone looked in my direction.

Once I'd observed the group and picked out my targets I slowly retreated 100 yards to a small bush growing on the open river bar. I ducked in behind it and clicked twice on the radio. Franz immediately turned on his light upstream of the group and began approaching them. He yelled out, "Fishery officers! Stay where you are!" It was like lighting a firecracker in a crowd, as the group scurried off in all directions.

I focused in on my first quarry. The one I really wanted started running right toward me. He was running full speed in the dark as he approached the bush I was crouched behind. I never said a word as he approached. I stood up at the same time he reached the bush, stretched my hand out and grabbed him by the arm. The startled poacher leapt about two feet off the ground as I hung on to his arm without saying a word. He let out one of the loudest farts I have ever heard; at least, I assumed it was a fart.

I identified myself as his feet touched down on the gravel bar and he began to shake like a heroin addict needing a fix. He stammered, "Excuse me!" That's hard to believe but his first words were "Excuse me." He followed that with, "I'm so glad it's you. I thought it was a bear!" By this time Franz had arrived and we took the man back to the stand to recover the fish, nets and packs. The rest of the group were gone but we had our main target.

We took him back to our truck to take a statement and issue an appearance notice. I had my trusty dog Smokey in the truck waiting and I decided to try something using the dog. I'd been given permission to use Smokey on the job to track people. I'd been working with him in the office by hiding a frozen salmon and having him find it. I'd only done this a few times but he loved the game. I took Smokey back to the river by the fishing stand and told him to find the fish. His ears perked up and his nose went down as he began tracking.

Smokey headed for the trees on the shore. I could see some wet footprints on the gravel so I knew that Smokey was on the trail of someone who'd probably been fishing. We followed the tracks into the trees and into very thick brush. I couldn't see any tracks but trusted Smokey's nose. He kept going deeper into the thicker brush and started climbing up a steep bank. Just when I began to doubt where my dog was leading me a voice yelled out, "Okay, okay, I'm coming out. Call off your dog!"

I pulled Smokey back on his leash as the man came toward us. He was quite a sight! His arms were all scratched, there were a few tears in his clothes and he had only one shoe on. "Have you seen my other shoe?" he huffed. "No sir, I haven't." He then reached down and took the other shoe off, heaved it deep into the brush and said, "This one won't be doing me much good either then." Smokey and I walked the shoeless poacher back to the truck where Franz would deal with him while I looked for more.

I returned to the river and Smokey got on another trail. He went into the bush and I heard something else. "Get him Smokey!" I knew Smokey wouldn't bite unless someone hit him but I thought it would get the hidden foe moving or make him surrender. Then I heard some strange screaming: Smokey had found himself a cat.

Smokey hadn't liked cats ever since the mother-in-law's cat scratched him on the nose when he was a puppy. Smokey grabbed that cat and shook it, and it ran away from the in-laws never to be seen again.

I went into the bush and shone my light on the noise. White cat hair was flying everywhere. It was a blur of activity. I yelled at Smokey to come back as he had given this cat a full skeleton massage. The cat managed to scramble up a tree and I pulled Smokey back. I felt bad for the cat—sort of. I don't really like cats and I wished it'd been another poacher. I decided to leave the area with the two poachers we had.

This poaching story became well known in the community. A friend of mine was an auxiliary with the RCMP. I'd joined the auxiliary program in the Nass to work with the RCMP and educate them about our job as well as learn about police work in the community. The poachers I encountered were often the same people police dealt with. A fellow auxiliary called me up one night with a funny story. He'd been at a party and heard about the chase from the people we'd caught. It turned out there were a number of women in the group as well. One of then had taken her white cat to the river. I was pleased to learn the cat survived after a trip to the vet. One of the girls was hidden in the brush and I nearly stepped on her as I walked past. She was terrified and thought she'd be going to jail.

Others in the group relayed their terrifying ordeal. One young man had run over three miles to a nearby house and waited until morning before knocking on their door and calling for a ride. It sounded like they were terrified enough to not try it again.

The two we'd caught were charged and fined $400 each.

The polite poacher turned out to be a university student attending Saskatchewan University in Saskatoon. He just happened to be in the same program in which my wife's best friend worked as a lab assistant. Lorraine told her the story and apparently she approached the poacher in the hallway one day and said, "I hear you're quite a fisherman!" He turned red in astonishment, wondering how she could possibly know about something that had happened 1,000 miles away two weeks earlier.

I've often thought about the series of events that night and wondered what I'd have done in the same circumstances. I'm quite sure if I was running full speed through the dark and was grabbed by something the first words from my month would not be, "Excuse me!" He truly was one of the politest poachers ever.

Ants in My Pants

Tom Moojalsky was the senior enforcement manager from Vancouver who loved to come out to the field and work with fishery officers whenever he could find time. He heard about the fun I was having in Quesnel and decided to come up and participate. It was always good to have some help, and Franz and I enjoyed the support.

I took Tom out to check on some fishing sites during the day for signs of activity. *Mantracker* had nothing on us. We deployed various methods and tactics to determine if and when people had recently been in the area because no one drives or walks to the river without leaving some sort of visual clues.

We walked down a trail near town and saw signs of recent activity. We arrived at the river to find a set gillnet. It was a bit strange that someone was setting an illegal net in broad daylight and we decided we should leave the net and return after dark to catch the culprits. Just as we started up the bank we heard someone approaching us from the trail. Tom and I scurried back to the riverbank to lie down on the ground where we could see the gillnet. Our intention was to watch the poacher come down to check his net, then arrest him. The plan worked perfectly as the

Franz and I patrolled the Fraser River by jet boat near Quesnel, checking for illegal nets and fishing sites for signs of criminal activity.

man cautiously approached the riverbank and looked around in all directions. We couldn't move because we were lying on some very crunchy noisy leaves but we were patient and willing to wait as long as it would take. That was until we realized we were lying on an ant pile. Ants were crawling all over both of us as we lay there not moving a muscle. We were so close to the net that we would certainly be heard if we moved. Waiting for the poacher to check his net seemed like an eternity

He had two small children with him as well, presumably to teach them how to catch Chilcotin turkeys, and he was in no hurry as he sat on the bank and had a smoke. About thirty minutes passed; he finally stood up, pulled the net in and took eight sockeye out before resetting it. By now ants had found their way onto just about every part of our bodies you can imagine.

With the poacher now cooked we quickly stood up and approached him. He tried to run but had nowhere to go, making the chase a non-event, and he co-operated from that point on. He looked at both of us curiously as we squirmed and wriggled all the while we were dealing with him.

We were just cleaning things up on the riverbank when I looked across the river and saw another group of people at the river on the opposite shore. Tom and I quickly dealt with the net, fish and poacher, and then drove the half hour around to the other side of the river to try catching more poachers.

It was dusk and still somewhat light out as we started walking down the trail where we'd seen the poachers. We hadn't gone 100 yards when we saw someone coming up the trail. We quickly stepped off the trail and waited as the two approached carrying heavy packsacks. When they were right beside us, Tom and I stepped out with Smokey on a leash and no one ran. They had thirty sockeye in their packs. We took them back to the truck and gave them all a coupon.

I realized they didn't have a net with them so I ran down to the river to check the fishing site. I arrived at the riverbank to find two more people fishing. This was too easy! I didn't try a sneak approach this time though. I looked down at the two of them from directly above. They looked up and although I was in uniform they didn't react. I thought I'd try something. "Hi guys. Oh, it's just you. I saw someone else up here and I wasn't sure who it was." They watched in bewilderment as I climbed down the bank.

One then tried to run but lasted only fifty yards. I escorted the two of them back to the truck where Tom was waiting. We'd just caught three different groups of poachers in about an hour. Welcome to the Cariboo! The poaching was so rampant people were willing to fish in daylight. That was changing quickly though as word was getting out about officers that worked at night and one of whom ran people down.

A New Administrative Assistant

T he paper workload was taking far too much of my field time; the more poachers I caught the more paperwork I had. I'd raised my concerns numerous times at our meetings, as had other officers. It just didn't seem logical to have field officers spending so much time on paperwork. There goes that logical thinking again! In government, sometimes you have to be creative and try another method.

I was merrily typing away in my office one day, trying to complete the court documents before heading out on patrol to look for more "clients," when I paused and said to myself, "This paper-work is unbearable. How can I convince my supervisor I needed some admin support? Unbearable! That's it!"

Maybe it was the lack of sleep or the boredom of typing that had triggered my idea. I went into the warehouse and opened the freezer. There lay a frozen roadkill black bear that the conservation officer had asked me to store until it could be disposed of. I lifted the frozen bear from the freezer and packed it into my office. It was frozen in a pose that allowed me to seat it in an office chair. I placed a fishery officer patrol cap on the bear and rolled the chair up to the typewriter and then I asked the conservation officer to

Lack of sleep spawned the idea to pose with a frozen, roadkill bear and send the picture to the boss pleading for an administrative assistant—it worked!

take a picture of me instructing my new "admin employee." He laughed so hard he couldn't hold the camera still but he finally snapped a few pictures before I put the bear back in the freezer.

I took the same detailed cost-analysis document I'd previously sent to my supervisor and attached my bear photo along with a note stating I'd hired an administrative assistant. I forwarded a couple of copies to a few other key supervisors. Two weeks later I was given authority to hire a real part-time administrator.

Changing Attitudes

I needed to get the courts' support before I could expect any change in attitude toward poaching. I decided to try educating the judge about the impacts of poaching. I wrote an impact statement to present in court the next time poachers appeared. I also made out twenty-one first appearance notices for the court date on which I planned to introduce the impact statement.

The judge entered the packed courtroom of twenty-one poachers and me. He couldn't hide his bewilderment at the number of people present. The Crown lawyer advised him he had twenty-one first appearances for illegal fishing. The first poacher on the court list was called forward and entered a plea of guilty. The Crown read the impact statement and the judge listened intently.

The standard fine for poaching had been a standing joke in the community as people were getting a maximum of a $75 fine. Things changed that day as the judge fined each of them $400 to $500. Word spread fast throughout town. The media wanted to talk to me. The local radio and newspaper began covering the poaching stories in the news. The whole town was abuzz. I also knew I could expect twenty-one fewer Christmas cards next December.

The media frenzy in Quesnel was growing so I took a newspaper reporter on patrol one night. We caught several poachers and he wrote a full-page article about the evening.

The local RCMP officer in charge of the Crime Stoppers program approached us and suggested we run a story about poaching. I thought it was a brilliant idea. Over the next week we put together a TV commercial and articles in the paper and we had posters printed. The posters were put up around town and at some strategic fishing locations along the river.

We continued to catch poachers but now we were being asked about the Crime Stoppers program by those we caught. Of course the program was confidential and we would not disclose any details about it. This uncertainty became a huge deterrent factor; poachers weren't trusting each other for fear their fellow fish thieves might turn them in for some quick cash.

In one illegal sales case we caught two men selling fish through an undercover operation. The very next day we caught the same two guys again. They both thought their partner in crime had ratted on them for the cash. In this case we had caught them without any help but we didn't tell them that.

It was entertaining watching their reactions when I interviewed them and advised them we couldn't disclose any information from the Crime Stoppers program. One threatened me, "If I catch you on the river I'll blow your f#%@& head off." I knew we were having an impact on his illegal business and knew I'd have to be extra cautious around him.

The two fish sellers eventually had a big fight and parted ways. One officer with a dark sense of humour even suggested we send each of them a cheque from Crime Stoppers but mail the cheques to the other one's address. We never really considered following through but it sure would have been entertaining. We'd found the program to be another successful tool that we utilized many times.

The attitude toward poaching was starting to change. We noticed a slight drop in numbers and we were getting feedback through the media that people were not as willing to talk about it. People breaking the law do not want media exposure. I made sure reporters received any information I could provide them. The media were a valuable tool that I would use in every community I worked in.

September arrived too quickly my first summer in Quesnel. It had been a crazy season for poaching—we had charged over seventy poachers and every single one had tried to run when we arrived. There were at least another 250 to 300 people on the river who were undoubtedly involved, but who could not be charged due to lack of evidence.

The media coverage, the Crime Stoppers program and the increased severity of sentences in the courts all seemed to be making a small dent in the poaching. Nonetheless, when we took a helicopter flight in late August to check a number of areas we located forty active fishing sites along the Fraser River, found three gillnets set in the Quesnel River and also located an operating suction dredge.

A suction dredge is essentially a vacuum cleaner that sucks up rocks, gravel, fish and anything else smaller than the diameter of the intake nozzle. The material is poured through a sluice box to remove gold and then dumped back into the river. They are illegal to operate in BC but some are willing to take the chance for the lucrative reward.

We landed the helicopter, stopped the operation, seized all the equipment and left an appearance notice with the two operators. They were rather surprised when we landed and immediately thought someone had reported them for Crime Stoppers cash. Of course we couldn't disclose that information! They were convicted in court and fined $800 and all the gear was forfeited.

With the success of Crime Stoppers and increased enforcement, poachers began looking for new areas to fish as we caught more and more of them in their favourite spots. Some would look for remote places difficult to access in hopes we wouldn't find them. Still others took the bold move of intimidating First Nations fishers at their fishing sites.

I received more than one report about poachers threatening

First Nations fishermen. They would scare them off and use their fishing sites to poach. I was able to investigate these incidents and bring criminal charges against those responsible. The poachers in the Cariboo truly were a tough lot to change.

Instead of chasing off local First Nations fishermen, other poachers tried a different strategy, which I observed at a fishing site thirty miles south of Quesnel on the Fraser River.

I'd crawled into a fishing site and located a group of fishers, consisting of three young men and two young women. I learned that two of them were from the local First Nations band and could be fishing legally. Poachers would often try to fish with a First Nations person in the belief that I wouldn't catch them. They would simply stop fishing and pass the gear to the legal fisherman if I came along. It was a good idea except I wouldn't come in until I observed everyone fishing from some secret vantage point.

Lying in the dark on the riverbank directly above their fishing site, I could hear all the conversation in the group. They talked about the new sneaky fishery officer in town. "You never know where he is and he walks around in the dark. He's almost like a ghost." I barely managed to contain my laughter as I emerged from the bushes.

Hatfields & McCoys

I received an anonymous handwritten letter one day reporting illegal sockeye in the freezer of a rural resident. I knew the farmer and suspected I knew who the anonymous writer was. This was a case of a neighbourhood rift. We were so busy it took a week to validate the information and secure a search warrant for the residence on the island.

Eventually I took another officer in a small boat to visit the farmer. Sockeye were found in the freezer but it was evident that a much larger quantity had been stored and removed before we arrived. Charges were still laid and the farmer went into a frothing rage. He was another politically connected person who was used to pushing the provincial authorities around. He was saddened to learn I worked for the federal government and that his connections were futile in his efforts to have charges dropped.

This same farmer had gone to considerable lengths to obtain authority for a permanent roadway across a large side channel of the Fraser River. There was zero chance such an approval would be given for a number of reasons: the side channel was vital in high water to disperse the water; fish spawned in the side channel; and a road or dike would not hold in high water. At least that's what an expert and anyone thinking clearly would conclude. A costlier bridge would be the only plausible option.

I thought the issue was over until I received an anonymous tip that I should drive down and check the property out. I drove the forty minutes to the farm and was shocked! Two D-8 Cats, a D-6 Cat and a twelve-yard earthmover were busily building a dam/causeway across the side channel of the river using river gravel. Anyone with common sense could see the causeway would not hold. It was like building a dam out of marbles.

My first task was to stop the construction. I approached a Cat operator and was directed to a pickup truck to meet the boss, who turned out to be the farmer. I'm not qualified to diagnose human rabies, but his lengthy tirade made me concerned about his health. He was a physically imposing figure but I knew he couldn't run a five-minute mile so I stood still and tried to appear calm. He was totally irrational and his emotions had taken over. I empathized with his predicament of being unable to access his home easily. I finally had to say something to get his attention and said, "Was this not an issue when you bought the property?" I knew I should have chosen better words. I was then subjected to another ten minutes of entertainment before I was able to determine that the equipment belonged to his friend.

The farmer's threats were getting serious and the fact I was alone at the time caused me to leave and get help. I returned two hours later with a conservation officer and two staff from the provincial Water Management Branch.

I walked over to the owner of the equipment and recognized him as someone I'd curled against. I also knew he had very large arms and a fairly quick temper. I was direct and concise with the conversation. "This equipment has to stop construction right now or it will all be seized." He knew me well enough to know I wasn't bluffing and immediately ran over and stopped all the equipment.

I went back to the rabid farmer. He must have received some medical attention as his demeanour had improved. He understood he had gone too far and knew his political connections would be of no assistance. I took some information from him and the equipment operators before driving home to devise a plan for the causeway removal.

The conservation officer and I returned to the site armed with a single shovel. The roadway was over 20 feet high, 200 feet long and 50 feet wide at the base. The rising spring flood waters were lapping at the crest on the upstream side while the downstream side was almost dry except for some leakage through the porous gravel. We didn't venture too far onto the causeway for fear it could collapse and wash away at any time.

We initiated our plan with the shovel, digging a small trench on the upstream side to allow a trickle of water over the top of the causeway. Then we stood back and marvelled at the power of water. Within a minute the water was flowing wider and moving the loose gravel. It only took a couple more minutes before the rumbling started. It sounded like a jet taking off and the entire causeway was gone in about five minutes! Thousands of yards of gravel disappeared into the river downstream. It was an unbelievable sight.

The farmer did eventually get proper approvals and finally constructed a bridge across the side channel.

The Warning Shot

It was important to try to apprehend poachers before they reached their vehicles. Current policies limit car chases but I had more than a few while working in Quesnel.

One normal evening patrol had netted a few poachers and we were checking one more site before the sun rose. We turned down a road and drove with our headlights out to avoid detection. We were a mile from the site when we noticed the headlights of a vehicle coming up from the river. We waited until he was close before turning our emergency lights on to stop him.

The driver swerved the car to the right and drove around us, spinning gravel and dust in all directions. I turned our vehicle around and made chase through the blinding dust storm ahead. When the car reached pavement it headed for town and four miles later it turned onto a side road. I came around a curve on a narrow gravel road to see the car stopped in front of a large dead-end berm of dirt.

The driver had bailed out of the running car and disappeared into trees over the bank. I pulled up close behind the car just as I noticed it rolling back toward me. The driver had left the car running and the driver's door was open. The car rolled back before stopping against the front bumper of my truck.

I jumped out of the truck with Smokey and chased after the driver while the other officer agreed to stay with the vehicles and call for a tow truck. I ran down the road to the point we'd seen the man disappear into the trees. In my haste to run him down I had forgotten my flashlight and didn't have time to go back.

I stepped off the road where the man had disappeared and slid about six feet down a steep bank. This was no small step for mankind! Smokey was running ahead of me hot on the trail of the fishy-smelling driver and I could hear noisy steps as the driver ran through the trees.

I had almost caught up when things went totally silent. I stopped and looked around. The moonlight made it possible to see the outline of trees but I couldn't see anything else. I started thinking I should go back for a light because I didn't know who I was chasing. He might be armed. I stood quietly pondering my next move. I slowly stepped forward toward the spot where I'd last heard noise and I heard Smokey whining about thirty feet ahead.

I called Smokey back and stared in vain into the dark. "I should have eaten more carrots as a child," I thought. I was ready to go back to the truck for a light when I happened to look up, and there I saw the silhouette of a person fifteen feet up a small poplar. He was clinging to the small tree with his arms and legs locked around it in a ball, doing his best impersonation of a burl.

I took Smokey by the collar and walked forward until we were directly under the tree. I needed to have some fun with this one and said, "Smokey, I don't know where he went. I'm going to fire a warning shot up into the trees and see if we can get him running again." A panicked voice above us said, "Don't shoot! I'm right here! I'll come down! Please don't let the dog bite me!"

I was laughing inside as the sheepish poacher slithered down from his lofty perch to my waiting handcuffs. I walked the man back to my truck and partner. The tow truck was on its way.

We seized two nets and twenty-five sockeye from the trunk of the car before turning the car over to the tow-truck driver. High-speed chases are dangerous and this poacher was treated seriously. We took him to the RCMP to be held until the next day for a court appearance. We learned he was one of the biggest drug dealers in the area and considered violent. His car, fish and net were forfeited and he was convicted of fishing and driving violations.

Fun and Follies at the Ferry

A cable ferry south of Quesnel on the Fraser River was a favourite fishing site. It had easy access and the fishing success was high, which made it a great spot to patrol. One night I watched a fisher catch 200 sockeye in an hour with a dip net.

I had to approach the ferry in the dark to avoid detection. I'd park a half mile away some nights and walk into the site to watch. On one of those nights I reached the site just as a group who'd been fishing on the ferry got into their truck to leave. I knew I couldn't get back to my truck in time to return so I sprinted across the landing in hopes of getting to them before they started the truck.

I forgot about the steel cables that held the ferry structure to the bank. As I reached full speed the cable caught me just below the knee and launched me through the air. "So this is what it must feel like to be Superman," I thought, before I hit the ground and did a complete somersault. I couldn't believe my good fortune—no broken bones and no sprained joints, just a two-inch scrape across my left shin.

I started running toward the truck again just as they pulled away. I hate to see one get away but there was nothing I could do. I walked over to the spot where they'd been parked and looked around. My good fortune lay on the ground: a driver's licence had fallen from someone in the truck.

I returned to my truck and drove to the residence on the driver's licence to find three guys cleaning fish in the open garage. I approached the one I recognized from the driver's licence and said, "It was a good night at Marguerite Ferry, wasn't it? You should be more careful about what you leave lying around," as I handed him his driver's licence. That was too easy.

The officers from Vancouver arrived again. I had them patrol areas that were easy to approach while I patrolled some of the more obscure sites. They called from the ferry one night and said they were chasing a truck. I was about three miles away and I quickly made my way to join the chase.

The officers were in hot pursuit but, as we later learned, the truck had some kind of high-performance engine and it was pulling away on them. Nonetheless, they were able to spot a sockeye salmon falling out the back of the truck onto the side of the highway. The officers were losing the chase but they saw the truck turn sharply up a side road up ahead and they were able to follow. They rounded a curve to find the truck stopped on the road with smoke pouring from the engine.

Fate was on our side. I arrived just as they pulled up behind the truck, where the two men were standing cursing at the loss of their high performance engine. One sockeye had cost them several thousand dollars before the case even got to court. At trial the driver was fined $2,000 and given a one-year driver's licence suspension. At least he'd have time to rebuild the engine before he needed it.

It was still my first summer in Quesnel and I'd already had a career-full of experiences. I was starting to catch some people a second time. I'd caught one particularly large poacher in early July without incident but as we left him with his appearance notice he mumbled, "Next time you catch me one of us is going in the river!"

It wasn't enough evidence to charge him for threats and I

wondered if and when we might meet again. As fate would have it we did meet again, on August 25. It was another patrol to the ferry landing that located this behemoth of a mountain man and two of his friends.

He was fishing as Tom and I approached him. I shone my flashlight at him and told him who I was. I made sure I had a good escape route because I didn't want to get too close to King Kong until I knew things were safe. His two buddies had fled. The guy was not happy to see me again. He clenched his fists, hissed through his teeth and glared into the light. I took a dry gulp and asked him to come back to the truck. He looked around like a caged animal without saying a word. "Come back to the truck and let's deal with this. Don't do anything stupid or you'll get into more trouble," I suggested, hoping he'd forgotten his promise earlier in the summer.

Then he turned his back to me. That's not a good thing. I placed my hand on the butt of my gun because I didn't know if he was reaching for a weapon. "Show me your hands!" I ordered. He raised his hands above his head but kept his back to me and waded out into the river. He went in up to his hips and then dove forward into the very cold, fast-flowing Fraser River. I could only think of his promise earlier in the summer and I was sure glad it was him going into the river and not me.

As the man swam into the darkness and quickly drifted downstream my attention turned to concern for his safety. The current was so fast and the water so cold that he couldn't survive for long. I knew the river current moved away from the shore and downstream was dangerous water.

I screamed at him to swim toward shore. He was about a hundred yards upstream from the reaction ferry docked parallel to the shore. I ran along the shoreline and kept yelling at him to swim toward me. He soon realized how dumb his decision had been and was desperately trying to swim back to me. "Head for the ferry," I yelled.

I ran downstream and scrambled up onto the ferry with Tom

just as the poacher disappeared underneath the front of it between the twin hulls. We ran to the downstream end of the ferry and lay down on the deck waiting for him to appear. He didn't come out! We could hear some thumping under the metal hulls and thought he might be caught up underneath.

I hung my head over the side and shone my light upstream into a pair of fearful eyes. He was hanging onto a metal support that ran between the two hulls of the ferry about twenty feet from my reach. The current was so strong his whole body was stretched out on the surface of the river.

I wasn't sure what to do but I did know the guy weighed well over 200 pounds and I was only 155. He was getting very tired and had to let go of the support but managed to grab the next one. He worked his way toward us in this way until he was hanging onto the last support, right below us. If he let go of this one he'd be swept into the darkness downstream. Tom and I decided we'd try grabbing him.

This was a tough decision because we knew his size and knew that if he struggled we could both end up in the river too. We each grabbed an arm and pulled. The man didn't struggle at all. He was totally exhausted and could neither fight nor help us. Somehow we managed to pull the soaked man from the river and up onto the ferry deck. We lay there gasping for air before helping him onto his feet.

We took the shivering Hulk to our truck and drove him back to town. He was coherent (well, as coherent as an idiot who would jump into the Fraser River at night could be) and warm by the time we reached town. We took him home and he thanked us when we charged him. He never went poaching again.

Dumb and Dumber

Most poachers were trying to change their tactics to elude us. This made the hunt more of a challenge and we always tried to keep ahead of them, but there were a few tactics that defied all logic.

I was asked to plan night patrols for a few senior managers coming to visit the area. They wanted a firsthand view of the poaching free-for-all. Franz and I picked a few active sites close to town for the visit. We purposely didn't patrol them for a while beforehand to increase the chances of catching poachers when the brass visited.

My supervisor and two managers from Vancouver joined Franz and me for their first night patrol. We walked down the railroad tracks to check one site that we hadn't visited in three weeks. We were all standing on the tracks and Franz and I were explaining how we'd approach the site when we noticed two people walking down the tracks toward us in the dark. One of the two had a dip net over his shoulder. We greeted them politely and watched in amazement as they walked right on by two uniformed fishery officers and down to the fishing site. I thought we'd caught the dumbest poachers before but these two men might have just learned to walk upright!

The rest of the crew waited above on the railroad tracks while I crawled down the boulder-strewn bank before getting close to the two. They'd already caught some fish. I was within ten feet of the poachers when I stood up, turned my light on and grabbed the closer one. I started putting him in handcuffs and the other one started running away. "Yahoo, I get to run another one down!"

The guys on the tracks above were able to move along the flat railroad bed as the poacher and I scrambled through the large boulders. My boss on the tracks yelled, "Okay, let the dog loose!" We didn't have a dog but I can do a fairly good dog impression so I started barking.

My boss yelled at the poacher again, "Oh come on, you can do better than that!" I closed the gap quickly, slowed down behind the poacher and said, "Nice night for a run, eh?" I tried not to laugh when I caught the guy shortly after. "Where's the dog?" he queried. "Woof! Woof!" I responded. "You're kidding!" Shamefaced, he shook his head.

The poacher had stopped running because he thought he might sprain an ankle on the rocks. He claimed to be a three-hour marathon runner. "That's not fast enough for around here," I said. "I run in the low 2:30s." I put my second pair of cuffs on him and helped him up the bank to the waiting officer and managers. The poachers had to put up with our gut-busting laughter (and my occasional growling) all the way to the truck.

City of Quesnel in Poop

I was attacking the loads of paperwork one day when I received a phone call reporting a fish kill in Baker Creek in Quesnel (Baker Creek is a salmon stream flowing right through town). I took my sample kit and headed to the creek.

Dead fish were floating everywhere in the stream. Everything from small trout and fry to adult pink salmon was floating among the raw sewage, condoms, tampons and "brown trout." I gathered samples and pictures as I followed the crap upstream to the city sewage treatment yard.

The plant had experienced problems in the past and the city had been directed to fix it. This was the Cariboo though, and the environment was not a high priority for the city council in the 1980s. I took statements from city staff and concluded they'd directed untreated sewage into the creek while they changed a line. The spill had run for twelve hours before they stopped it and thousands of fish had died in the stream.

The media were all over the spill. I couldn't disclose the facts until charges were laid but the local mayor went on a personal attack of me. He was quoted in the paper as calling me "a federal bureaucrat out witch hunting," and blaming me personally for the case against the city.

I didn't take it personally and felt confident in the case. If the city and staff had tried to work with us rather than attack us the problem could have been solved sooner.

A Vancouver prosecutor handled the lengthy trial in which the city tried to claim a vandal had broken into their treatment facility and turned some valves, releasing chlorine in the creek. "Someone's been holding their breath way too long," I thought. We proved that even if that were true the city employees were negligent by not having the facility locked. The doors had locks that hadn't been used in many years.

The case was dismissed but the Crown appealed and the city was convicted. I told the prosecutor that the conviction on the City of Quesnel was as good as sex; he told me I was a sick man. The city was ordered to fix the problem and fined $6,500. The mayor took me off his Christmas card list for a time. Happily, in later years the mayor realized his disregard for the environment was dated, even for the Cariboo, and became a "born-again environmentalist." We were able to resolve future issues cordially.

Kinky Poacher

Together with another officer I served a warrant on a resident in Quesnel. A disgruntled neighbour had reported him, indicating he had a large quantity of sockeye in his freezer. The officer and I arrived at the residence around 5 p.m. expecting the man to be home from work.

I knocked on the door and no one answered but we could hear noises from inside the house, so someone was home. The other officer ran around to the back of the house in case they tried to remove fish out the back door. I pounded on the door again and the owner finally opened the door.

I handed him the warrant and he nervously read it before allowing us to enter. We began our search in the obvious places like the fridge and the freezer. One fresh sockeye was found in the fridge and the freezer contained a large amount of other meat and food but no fish. However, I could see from the blood and fish scales that fish had been lying in the bottom of the freezer.

We knew he'd had time to hide some fish and we started a more detailed search. It reminded me of an Easter egg hunt as a kid! I found a bag of fish stuffed in a corner of the furnace room and two more sockeye were found in the wood stove. I told him I didn't think sockeye would keep his house warm.

We found several more salmon as we searched the house. I went into the master bedroom and looked under the bed. I put my hand on the bed when I knelt down and felt something under the covers so I threw them back to find another frozen sockeye. The poacher said, "Hey, I'm a kinky guy. Is there a law against sleeping with a fish?" At least he had a sense of humour—until I told the judge the details of the search. He was fined twice as much as other poachers.

Cuffed to a Tree

The second summer in Quesnel started where the previous year left off. I was more prepared and knew the trails but the poachers were also more prepared. They'd hide vehicles, walk farther into sites, set up tripwires with cans (to both trip us up and signal our approach), have a person watching the trail or even set up a deadfall, a large tree propped up with a tripwire, designed to fall on us when we came down the trail. Poaching was serious business.

Tom and I checked one last trail at 4 a.m. one July morning just as daylight was breaking. Two poachers carrying packsacks were walking toward us on the trail. When they saw us they flung off their packs and headed off into the trees. I was ready for an early morning run and took off after them, leaving Tom with the packs of fish.

These two guys were in better shape than most. They weren't following any trail as they sprinted through the mature pine forest. I caught the first poor wheezing soul after five hundred yards. I could still see his partner running ahead of me but I had to deal with this guy first. I knew Tom couldn't get to me in time to catch the second guy so I handcuffed the poacher to a large pine tree. I looked around the area and up into the sky and said, "Gee, I hope I can find this place again!"

The second poacher had turned onto a trail that I followed for some time before realizing he had gone in the other direction. I backtracked to the trail junction and followed the footprints of the poacher. I eventually caught him and took him to our truck where Tom was waiting, and then I returned to the first poacher cuffed to the tree.

An hour had passed by the time I arrived back at the tree to find a most terrified poacher. The guy had freaked out! He had thought he'd heard a bear and had panicked. He'd torn the bark off the tree with the chain on the handcuffs as he desperately ran around it and the grass was ripped up around his feet. It looked as though two bears had been fighting. He was shaking with fear. I did feel sorry for him, but managed to get over it. He was so glad to see me and co-operated fully during the walk back to our truck.

I hadn't planned on being that long and nor did I expect him to react the way he did, but it was a funny story that made its way around DFO for years. However, the story came back to haunt me twenty years later in 2006. I was curling in the Brier with our BC team in Regina when I was approached by a reporter. He'd been talking to a BC reporter about my running career and work as a fishery officer. The conversation led to some of my poaching stories and this reporter wanted to hear a few.

I told him the story about the grizzly bear attack and the poacher cuffed to a tree, and the stories spread across Canada like bad flu. Most major newspapers covered the story and everyone was having a few chuckles. Everyone, that is, except some senior human resources manager with DFO in Ottawa. I fielded a call between games at the Brier from this concerned lady in Ottawa about the poacher I'd cuffed to a tree. Her concern was that this could be viewed as cruelty or abuse. I initially thought a friend was pulling a prank on me but she was dead serious. I said, "Do you realize this happened over twenty years ago when the Constitution was fairly new? I talked to the poacher later and he was fine. I'm playing in the Brier and I'm on leave; I don't need any distractions. If you have an issue with this, write me a letter—and have a nice day." I never heard from her again.

Sneak Attacks

Another crew of four officers from Vancouver arrived to help out for a few days. It was an ugly, rainy evening but I knew poachers would fish in bad weather too. I took the crew down a few trails until we located some action.

I left the other officers on the trail and crawled in to find four guys huddled around a small campfire under some tall trees near the riverbank. They took turns walking down to the river to check their gillnet.

I quietly crawled back to the other officers to devise a plan. It was a treat to have four other officers along, making the approach much safer. I agreed to crawl back near the fire and watch the group for a while longer. I told each of them to crawl to an agreed location to ensure we had them surrounded and I'd give one click on the radio as our signal.

I crawled along the forest floor to within thirty feet of the fire. I could almost keep warm while listening to them talk about fishing. They even talked about the sneaky fishery officer and I chuckled when they suggested he'd never come out on a rainy night like this. Surprise, surprise!

I thought one of the officers had stepped on some branches

when I heard some footsteps. One of the poachers at the fire jumped up and yelled, "Who's there?" Another poacher stepped out of the darkness on the trail, "Oh this spot is already taken." It turned out another group intended to use the site and happened to approach after we were hidden. They left and the four poachers continued their discussion.

I was getting bored with their conversation and gave the click signal on the radio. The other officers had all managed to get in position without being seen. I stood up, turned my flashlight on and announced, "Fishery officers, nobody move!" The other four officers all turned their lights on and the startled poachers sat in the glare of five flashlights. One said, "Holy shit! It's the SWAT team!" It really did look like a scene from a movie. We were all dressed in camo rain gear and had made a very calculated, co-ordinated move on them.

The arrest went without a hitch and all four appeared before the less-than-happy judge. We were still a long way from compliance, but fines continued to rise and poaching continued to drop.

My confidence and ability to approach poachers quietly in the dark were improving. I'd been given permission to wear running shoes rather than heavy hiking boots; the runners were lighter and quieter on the rocky banks of the rivers.

Two poachers were fishing off a dip stand near Quesnel and we'd observed them long enough to obtain evidence on both. I told the other officers I wanted to see how close I could get and started a slow crawl along the noisy rocks. I arrived on the shore end of their platform and they still hadn't noticed me. I stood up and tapped one on the shoulder.

The startled poacher jumped and yelled. His colleague turned as I identified myself and switched my light on. The other two officers quickly approached to help out. The fishermen were both a bit shocked that I'd managed to get so close without them knowing. I had to keep the ghostly reputation alive.

A similar situation found us approaching the dip stand of a First Nations fisherman. He had a dog lying on the shore end of the platform while he was fishing. "This should be challenging," I thought as I crawled along the rocks. I knew the dog would jump up at any moment but was amazed how close I was getting.

I reached the stand and stood up. The dog was asleep and didn't move as I quietly stepped over it and directly behind the guy fishing. I tapped him on the shoulder. He never jumped or hesitated. He slowly turned his head and looked at me, glanced down at his sleeping pooch and said, "I guess I gotta get a new dog, eh?" My laughter woke his dog.

The Man with the Axe

Our efforts to control illegal fishing were having an impact on fish sellers as well. A few of the hard-core sellers would fish whether the river was closed or not. DFO managed the various fish runs through timing the closures when a particularly weak stock was migrating through the area, but that wouldn't deter those set on making money through illegal fish sales. (Budget cuts and reduced fishery officer numbers today will no doubt make it easier for poachers to ply their trade. I'm sure politicians will spin it as increased opportunities for small business. The real losers will be the fish and those fishers who obey the rules.)

One such seller was a bad guy we had dealt with many times. Each encounter with him became more difficult and his anger increased every time we seized his fish and charged him. He lived about four hundred yards above the Fraser River along a major highway. The trail down to the river was steep and narrow. He wanted large amounts of fish and packing them up the trail behind his house was difficult so this seller often fished at other sites with easier access. He did use the site during closed times though because we had difficulty getting into the site without him knowing.

We decided to check his site during a closure one night. We parked a half mile away, walked through the trees behind his house and started down the trail. Our progress was very slow because we knew he'd probably be violent. We were about halfway down the trail when we heard two shotgun blasts from the house.

We later determined the shotgun was a warning for the guy fishing down at the river. Someone in the house had driven by our vehicle and wanted to signal the person fishing.

Shotgun blasts in the dark certainly get your attention. With renewed caution we travelled down the trail until we reached the river. The site showed recent activity with fresh fish and blood everywhere. Whoever had been fishing had eluded us through another trail. We weren't really interested in poking around in the dark for someone we felt might be armed and violent. We took the net and fish and left the area.

Two days later we paid the seller a visit in daylight. I was standing in the small porch attached to the house when he came through the door like a shot. I jumped aside to avoid being hit by the door. This put me in the corner of the porch while the guy stood in the doorway blocking my only access out. I could see my partner behind him.

The guy picked up an axe from behind the door and clutched it in both hands. I knew he was unlikely to be interested in chopping wood and I had to talk fast. I looked into his fiery eyes and tried to calm him down. I really don't remember all of what I said to him during this tense standoff but he did start to calm down and eventually lowered the axe.

I was fortunate to have learned another lesson without serious consequences. I should have knocked on the door and then stood outside the porch and waited. It's a horrible feeling to stare at an angry man holding an axe five feet away. Luckily for me, my career did not end that day and the accused was given thirty days in jail for threatening an officer.

Oar Wars in Gill Bay

August 23, 1986, was one of the darkest days of my thirty-five-plus years in enforcement. I'd heard about problems in the Native fishery near Chilliwack where DFO biologists had announced a total closure on the Fraser River. The local band was defying the closure and planning a large demonstration.

I was called from Quesnel to travel to Chilliwack and join a team of fishery officers being assembled to deal with the event. The RCMP was briefed on the situation but, as was their general practice at the time, avoided involvement in the incident to maintain a position of neutrality and peacekeeping. That has changed over time but in 1986 we were handling the event on our own.

Senior DFO staff from Vancouver and Ottawa directed our approach to the protest. Unfortunately most senior managers had neither knowledge of enforcement nor understanding of the consequences of their direction. That was the conclusion of most officers and every inquiry ever conducted on DFO, and it wouldn't change for another twenty years.

I joined over twenty fishery officers in the Chilliwack office on the afternoon of August 22. Initial instructions from Ottawa were to gather catch information only and not to deal with the fact that illegal nets were being used for fishing. They felt this softer approach might stop the demonstration (or perhaps the fish run might miraculously increase). The group of officers unanimously refused the task and were told to wait until the next day.

Officers waited until late afternoon before direction finally came to go on the river and seize illegal nets. It was decided collectively to approach sites cautiously and not to get involved in seizing nets from sites with large groups. The day's patrols resulted in many gillnets being seized along with hundreds of fish. Word from the Native community indicated that the following day would be a planned demonstration at Gill Bay.

Thirty-one fishery officers launched seven jet boats on the river on August 23 for a coordinated sweep. A local officer operated each boat, with officers unfamiliar with the area taking on other roles. I was designated to operate a video camera to capture the events on film.

The nets were being seized with minor resistance early on the patrol. However, a large group had gathered at Gill Bay. There were about fifty people on shore and another twenty to thirty in small aluminum boats defending their nets set in the river. Things turned ugly fast. Our boat was propeller-driven and ended up disabled with a net around the propeller. Several small boats quickly surrounded us. I continued filming until my camera quit from the buckets of water thrown at us.

As one officer was trying to push the net out of the propeller with a long pike pole, one of the small boats approached and two people grabbed the end of the pole and started pulling. I was concerned they'd pull the officer overboard or get the pole and use the point to attack us. We were also concerned they themselves might fall into the river, as none of them had life jackets on.

I grabbed an oar from our boat and yelled at them to let go of the pole. They shook their heads so I warned them again. They just kept pulling on the pole and the officer was leaning well over the side of our boat. I reached out and hit the two people on the fingers. They held on tight so I hit them again. I was reaching out to hit them again when I noticed one of the men standing holding a seven-foot oar above his head and swinging it toward me.

If I hadn't seen the oar coming it would have struck me on the head. I turned away as the oar narrowly missed my head but struck me squarely on the right shoulder. The blade of the oar smashed into several pieces when it hit me. I staggered back and fell against one of the boat seats in extreme pain.

The thought ran through my head, "I'm not going to fall down." A strange thought but I knew I had to help out and I did manage to continue until our boat was freed. We sped away to a chorus of cheers and a hail of rocks being thrown from the beach. I was propped against the side of our boat. Then I was struck by a fist-sized rock on the chest. It hit me squarely on my notebook and bounced into the boat.

I had entered this day as a camera operator and yet somehow managed to find myself in the only disabled boat and battling with the demonstrators. Of the thirty-one officers in seven boats I was the only one struck with a rock. I know I've had more serious close calls than any other officer. I also know I am one of the luckiest people alive.

I was flown by helicopter to a waiting truck and taken to the hospital. My shoulder was cracked but not broken. I was given a sling and told to take it easy for a couple of weeks.

Meanwhile, back on the river, the RCMP had arrived to appear in front of the media cameras. I'll never forget the feelings I had as I listened to the senior RCMP on TV state that they had been called in to keep the peace. At the time he was conducting that interview I was being assaulted on the water. I usually have the utmost respect for the RCMP but it bothered me that they were more interested in good media coverage than protecting a fishery officer from assault. Little did I know the games had only just started.

I phoned my wife from the hospital in case she saw the news and heard I'd been injured. I didn't sleep a wink that night, worrying about how close I'd been.

I was trying to deal with the event the next day. Running is a big part of my life and I didn't want the assailant to have the satisfaction of knowing I couldn't run. I had to go for a run so I took my sling off and did six miles. It was incredibly painful, as every step jarred my shoulder. I must have looked like a hunchback with a limp as I hobbled down the road. Despite the pain, it felt so good that I'd managed not to lose my ability to run.

The media coverage over the following weeks was unbearable. Native groups from across Canada were demanding DFO fire me. These calls were from groups that had never met me.

Fishery officers compiled search warrants for the TV stations that had been in the boats with the Natives. Media will rarely give up video footage voluntarily or they may not be called to the next planned protest. I know it's a fact of life with the media but it was hard to accept.

The warrants were served and all the original video was seized. That created another national story: mean fishery officers entering the offices of television stations and taking their videos. The videos were ultimately valuable evidence because they showed the incident from several angles.

DFO in Ottawa succumbed to the pressure from First Nations and was openly critical of the search warrants executed on the media. The fishery officers sent them a "no thank you" card. Few in Ottawa understood then, or understand today, how to lead an enforcement branch. The video seized during the searches proved to be critical evidence in the eventual trial and conviction for assault.

Senior managers were scurrying around trying to respond to criticism from the First Nations community. A senior manager called me directly by phone. He advised he'd be sending a letter by fax that he'd drafted and wanted me to sign and return. The fax was a letter from me that apologized for everything that had happened and a lot that never happened. I was floored. The audacity of this small-minded, overpaid man was unbearable. The letter contained few facts and his information had been taken primarily from the newspaper. I didn't hesitate to call him back. I had no idea if I'd have a job in the future and decided to record the conversation.

I phoned him up and said, "This letter is appalling and inaccurate. I will write a letter based on facts and evidence and return it to you." He wanted it in fifteen minutes. I sent my draft to him and called. He wasn't happy because I'd changed his letter. Apparently the facts were unimportant to him. The conversation was brief. I asked him if he was considering disciplinary action if I didn't sign it and he said he wouldn't rule it out. I said, "Well you can f#&% off!" and hung up.

I wondered if I could be employed as a logger. After all, I was the Bull of the Woods in Nass Camp. I never regretted my comments in that conversation.

I knew I'd made the right choice to hold honesty and facts above political convenience but I wasn't sure where to go for help. I called Don Aurel, a senior officer in the lower Fraser, for assistance and he stepped in to help correct and inform senior management. I called one senior manager I felt I could trust, Pat Chamut. I relayed the entire story to him and he advised me he'd take care of it. I never heard another word about the letter and thankfully the senior manager transferred back east. Pat also gave approval for me to pursue civil action against the newspaper that had erroneously quoted me, although I declined to pursue the matter and feed the media frenzy.

My sombre mood changed when I received a letter of commendation from the Hon. John Fraser, former minister of DFO. The letter meant so much at the time and still does today. Someone recognized I was going through a crisis and took the time to say something. John Fraser was the first to acknowledge my situation in the department; that's leadership.

I continued to write briefings for Ottawa every time a manager fielded a complaint from someone. I sent the same briefing and copies of videotapes four times because Ottawa couldn't find any of the previous ones I'd sent. I decided their fifth request was the last and stated so in my letter to them.

I copied the videotape for the final time at home on the weekend, but when the copying was complete the VCR went on to record the show on TV, a scene from *Sesame Street* with Big Bird showing Bert and Ernie a fish and explaining where the fish came from. I laughed until my stomach hurt and knew this was a sign from above. I sent the video to Ottawa complete with the *Sesame Street* scene and was never asked for another copy.

The fallout from this incident reached the bizarre stage. I had taken a week off work due to the pain I was experiencing and the time I needed to cope with it all. I had never taken a week off before and didn't fill out the leave form properly. My leave was denied and I appealed. The case was ruled in my favour after two years of banter, and the BS ended when Pat Chamut became involved. It was refreshing to know that people like Pat and Don showed support during this incident.

Two trials stemmed from the protest: one against the First Nations chief who'd assaulted me, and one for charges laid against me for assault. Nothing surprised me any more in this nightmare. The political pressures on the department and on government were driving the decisions being made.

I confirmed this during the trial against me for assault. I was fortunate enough to have all the video evidence of the assault. The judge hearing the case kept stopping the videos in court and trying to understand where the alleged assault was. The person who'd accused me was never even close to me. The judge ruled that the force I'd used on the two pulling on the pole was necessary.

I approached the Crown lawyer prosecuting the case during a break in the trial and asked how the Crown could approve laying assault charges when no evidence existed. "Well Randy, you must realize these charges were made for political reasons," was the response. The judge dismissed the case in minutes after I'd waited over twenty months for the trial. I was thankful that political pressures hadn't reached him too.

It was another lesson learned. Politics can influence charges, regardless of the evidence or the impact it might have on people's lives. That's the reality anyone in enforcement must live with.

The trial against the chief who struck me with the oar took place in Chilliwack. The judge who heard the case had recently transferred to Quesnel where I'd appeared in court a few times.

The chief was convicted of assault and fined $500. I was shocked at the small sentence and left the courtroom. I walked past a few Natives who'd been in the courtroom and heard one say, "It was worth $500 to get a crack at him." I had never met any of these men and they had no idea who I was. I think the media frenzy had created a mythical demon in their minds. They may have been surprised to know I worked closely with First Nations. I was disappointed that DFO had been drawn into a staged battle and promised myself to find better ways to deal with protests.

I drove to the airport for the return flight to Quesnel. I arrived an hour early and wandered around the airport where I bumped into the judge who'd heard the case. He offered, "Come on Randy, I'll buy you a beer." He had no idea the emotions I was experiencing but hey, a free beer got my attention.

I had never talked to a judge about a case and was surprised at his first question, "Well Randy, what did you think of the case today?" I thought, "Does he really mean that? What will he think if I unload?" I fell back on my instincts and hit him with honestly. "Well sir, frankly I thought the sentence was very light and offered no deterrent for those who choose to assault fishery officers." He paused and took a sip of beer before responding. "I thought about jail time but thought the Native community would be upset. Yeah, you're right. I should have put him in jail."

His response was so casual I was silent. I realized then that judges are only people too. They hear all kinds of horrible stories and have to make decisions many times a day that affect people. Each person they make a decision on has far more emotion and interest in the case that they do. I will always respect the judge for his frankness and insight—and the free beer.

The department provided support to take civil action against the chief who'd struck me. The degree of proof in a civil case is lower than in a criminal case. Given that the chief had been convicted in criminal court, my legal counsel thought it would be fairly easy to prove. I was rather surprised at the judge's comments during the hearing as he told me I had to expect to get injured in the type of job we did and he disallowed the claim. It would be over twenty years before I could finally deal with the matter properly.

The entire event, trials and aftermath were certainly life-changing experiences. In future years I would be in charge of officers called on to handle several similar staged protests. We handled them all without incident in a variety of ways, always trying to work with the First Nations rather than against them. Some of the success stories appear later in this book.

I never did meet the chief who assaulted me and I truly regret that. He drowned about twenty years later when his fishing boat capsized and he was never found. I heard about the incident one morning when I awoke and turned on the radio. When I felt nothing, I knew this was wrong and wanted to do something.

I phoned a First Nations friend of mine, Charlene Belleau, and told her about it. She quickly arranged a healing circle with the current chief (brother of the deceased) and the daughter of the deceased. I was somewhat skeptical of the whole event but willing to try a new approach. The healing circle does not place blame on anyone; it simply provides both sides with a timely opportunity to share their feelings and discuss the impact on their lives. I will not discuss the specifics of what was said in the circle because that would be breaching the spirit of the event, and a promise made at the time, but I left the circle at peace with the entire incident and grateful to Charlene for arranging it. Our court system rarely allows such face-to-face, heartfelt discussions.

The circle certainly changed my feelings toward the event in a positive way and drove me to make changes in our agency to follow similar practices, such as restorative justice. Months later I had the opportunity to meet with two prominent leaders from the community. I had an open discussion with Ernie Crey and Doug

Kelly where we agreed to move forward and work together. There are still many people in DFO and in First Nations communities who aren't ready to take these steps. However, I truly believe they will eventually. I became a strong believer in the use of restorative justice to resolve conflict and I promoted the process throughout the rest of my career.

Pulp Mill Poachers

The Cariboo Pulp Mill, located on the bank of the Quesnel River, was a site where I'd previously found evidence of people fishing illegally. On one night patrol I noticed activity while watching from across the river so I drove around to the mill and went to their security gate. The attendant was reluctant to let me in and made a few phone calls before allowing us through.

I suspected he might have alerted the mill employees at the river. My suspicions were confirmed at the river, where there were obvious signs of recent activity. They'd even used a large loader to level the gravel out to the water's edge for easy access.

How could I catch these guys? I arranged a meeting with the mill manager, who listened intently as I made him an offer he couldn't refuse. He understood we could seize any equipment that had been used while committing an offence. The manager sent a stinging notice to all staff advising them that anyone caught fishing on mill property would immediately be fired. The mill also built an eight-foot chain-link fence along the river to prevent any employees from gaining access to the river. That was an easy fix by a responsible company. The mill manager later told me the fence also reduced theft from their facility. It turned out some employees were taking more than sockeye out the back of the property.

Duck! It's a Merganser!

The officers from Vancouver and I arranged a night patrol by boat. We were finding less poaching activity but the poachers we were finding were more likely to be hardened criminals. We planned to try a nighttime drift on the Fraser River that would be supported by a vehicle travelling downstream along the roads, but first we did a little research.

It was still daylight when another officer and I drove into a ranch yard we suspected was allowing poachers access to the river. We drove through the yard and down the two-mile dirt trail to the river, where we found recent signs of activity. We decided to check it later.

We drove up from the river and were stopped by an unoccupied pickup truck parked across the road to prevent our exit from the ranch. We cautiously got out and looked around. We called the RCMP dispatch to determine the owner and were not surprised to find it belonged to an extremely dangerous criminal known to assault police officers. The truck had been parked to send a message to us and I didn't like the message. I left my business card on the seat before we put the truck in neutral, pushed it aside and drove by.

We carried on the patrol with a heightened awareness of who might be out tonight. The two officers in the boat drifted along using a newly acquired night vision scope to check sites along the river. A vague outline of the drifting boat was visible in the light of the full moon, causing some concern because a poacher might see the boat as well. Everything was going as planned until the officers neared the site of the ranch where we'd encountered the truck.

A panic call came over the radio from the officers. "Gary's been hit! By a duck! No, it's actually a merganser." The two officers had been drifting quietly along when a low-flying merganser struck one officer in the jaw and chest, nearly knocking him out. The injured bird dropped into the boat and flopped around until Gary grabbed it by the neck, gave it a little chiropractic adjustment and threw it in the river.

Gary later told us he thought a poacher from shore had shot him when the bird hit him. I'm sure the odds of getting hit by a merganser at 3 a.m. in the middle of the Fraser River are far less than winning the lottery so we suggested he buy a ticket. The night passed without any poachers located, although we did manage to catch some poachers on the ranch at a later date.

Genius Poachers

High-speed chases were becoming far too common. People didn't want their trucks seized and nor did they want to go to court for the high fines they'd receive. We chased a truck one evening and the speeding truck proved to be far faster than our patrol vehicle but we were able to read the licence plate before it pulled away. The driver threw something out the window during the chase and we went back to look for the item. After searching the tall grass in the dark for forty-five minutes we found a wallet belonging to the genius driver/owner of the truck.

We took the wallet to the RCMP. They phoned Jimmy the Genius the next day and told him someone had found his wallet and asked that he come in to pick it up. I waited in the RCMP office until Jimmy arrived and then I arrested him. He was charged for a series of serious driving offences and lost his driver's licence for three years.

We never did determine why Jimmy the Genius threw his wallet out the window. Did he have a stolen wallet in his truck and threw his own out by mistake? Did he mean to throw a bag of drugs out instead? Did he think he could drive faster with less weight in the truck? Oh well, he had three years to figure it out.

I was working as an auxiliary RCMP one evening patrolling the downtown area of Quesnel. It was a clear evening in early winter and the river activities were over for the year. I worked with the RCMP to assist them in exchange for the support they provided in the summer.

We were taking a drive down Main Street when I noticed a fisherman whom I'd caught earlier in the summer and who had failed to show up in court. The judge had issued a warrant for his arrest. The officer pulled the car over and I called George over to the car.

The RCMP officer told him there was a warrant for his arrest for failing to appear in court for a fisheries violation. I stood there in disbelief—the guy didn't recognize me. I would have some fun with this. We took George back to the cells.

I stood at the jail counter facing George with my name tag clearly visible on the front of my shirt and asked, "Who caught you?" George replied, "That Nelson guy." I tried to contain myself when I said, "Oh yes, I hear he's real sneaky too." The RCMP officer left the room before bursting into laughter. George responded, "Yeah, he snuck up on us a few times. We call him Casper because he's just like a ghost; he caught me twice." I couldn't carry on and had to leave the room for a good laugh too.

I figured George the Genius must have been related to Jimmy the Genius. It seemed apparent that a few years of chasing poachers had weeded out the smarter ones. I went back into the room to continue booking George into the cells. He never did realize I was Casper. Maybe I am a ghost!

Spawning Poachers

The Quesnel Reserve had several well-used fishing sites. People fishing were easily alerted if we drove in so I would always walk or run in first. On this night I was working with Robert Martinolich of Vancouver; he was a nice guy, just not a runner. The river was closed to First Nations due to conservation concerns.

I left Robert in the patrol vehicle and climbed down my own secret trail to the site known as Indian Rock to find two people fishing. I didn't think they'd go anywhere soon and I wanted to check the road access before calling Robert.

I ran the four hundred yards through the trees to find two other men loading fish into their car. One of them was saying, "We got forty. Not bad for a late start." I stepped out of the shadows and shone my light on them. I took their car keys and had them sit in the front seat. I put one man's hand through the steering wheel and handcuffed the two men together.

I called Robert and we quickly loaded the fish into our car and gave the two men an invitation to an open house—in court. We took some wires off the engine in case they had other keys and we called a tow truck. I told Robert I'd run ahead to get the other two fishing at Indian Rock but when I got there only one of them was still fishing at the site. I gathered the few fish and net he had and was starting back down the trail when Robert arrived. We walked another fifty yards toward our truck when I heard some rustling in the trees. Shining my flashlight in the direction of the noise I found the second fisher with a pile of sockeye lying on the ground. The noise I'd heard was a fish flopping on the dry leaves. How appropriate was that? That single sockeye may not have spawned but he was solely responsible for the poacher's arrest and probably saved a few of his buddies in the river.

Rain was pouring down the very next night as I climbed down the steep, slippery trail leading to Indian Rock. The site was fifty feet below a rock shelf, making viewing easy. I could see two people fishing and approached cautiously. As I neared the edge of the cliff I noticed a small tarp tied to a tree near the edge of the cliff and I could hear voices.

This fishing group had a lookout posted to watch for fishery officers. My goal would be to crawl quietly to the person under the tarp and arrest him without alerting the guys fishing. My plan worked and I managed to crawl under the tarp only to find two people lying on the ground facing each other. I reached out to tap the guy on the back when he said, "Oh, I love you! I want to sleep with you tonight!" I wasn't used to that kind of offer!

I nearly burst out laughing before a voice from the river yelled, "Come on down! It's your turn!" A second offer I hadn't heard before! Maybe these poachers were turning a corner; they wanted me to sleep with them and go fishing with them! Not flippin' likely on either count.

I quickly crawled away and back along the trail to share my story with another waiting fishery officer. We carefully approached the site to observe "lover boy" take his turn fishing before we arrested the entire group. We gave them the standard invite to the courtroom social later in the summer. It turned out lover boy was wanted for attempted murder and didn't go fishing for a long while.

No Gold This Christmas

It was two days before Christmas, I had just caught up with a pile of paperwork and I decided to go for an afternoon patrol north of Quesnel. I crossed the Cottonwood River on Highway 97 North and climbed the big hill from the river valley. I glanced down a side road and saw a parked pickup truck with fresh footprints leading away from it down the snow-covered road.

It could have been any number of activities but I decided to check it out. I walked through the deep snow for over a mile, climbing along the upper banks of the Cottonwood River. The tracks finally turned off and headed downhill toward the river where I could hear a small motor running. Surely no one would be dredging for gold in this salmon stream in the winter?

Suction dredging is deadly in streams where salmon have spawned. The mining blows the eggs out of the gravel and silts up the spawning beds, not to mention destroying the entire substrate in the stream.

I stood hidden in the trees and—sure enough—there were two men in full diving suits working a suction dredge in the Cottonwood River. I looked through the binoculars and recognized one of the two as someone I'd caught earlier in the summer dredging another stream. I walked right up to them before they noticed me.

They were so surprised I'm not sure their dry suits remained dry. They said, "Don't you ever take time off? We never dreamt you'd be working this time of year or walk into this spot." I took it as a compliment and made sure to pass that information on to the judge.

There wasn't much the two of them could say. They were caught and one had a previous conviction. I seized everything at the site, including their dredge, gold, dry suits, diving gear and tools. I loaded whatever I could carry and walked with them out to their vehicle. I told them I would give them a ride home because I was seizing their truck too. Merry Christmas!

It would have taken several days to dismantle and pack the dredge out from the river and it was two days before Christmas so I hired a helicopter to sling the gear out from the river. The two miners were convicted in court and received fines of $3,000 each plus forfeiture of $4,000 worth of gear.

A Fantastic Day!

I knew 1988 would be a great year. Lorraine was expecting our third child in January. Our two girls and I were excited as the January 20th due date approached.

In early January I was notified I'd been selected to receive the International Pogue-Elms Award recognizing outstanding achievement in fish and wildlife law enforcement. The award would be presented in Vancouver at the next international meeting. I was elated until they told me the date: January 20.

Things worked out in the end; Lorraine gave birth to our son, Darren, at 8:35 a.m. My parents were visiting and took care of our daughters while I caught a 1:30 p.m. flight to Vancouver.

The award ceremony was an outstanding experience. I was overwhelmed by the widespread recognition from so many agencies from around North America. The award was named after two game wardens in Nevada who were murdered by an insane recluse.

All the threats and close calls with poachers, the name-calling from the mayor, the ongoing stress associated with the Gill Bay event, the late-night patrols seemed so worthwhile. Later in my career I always remembered the satisfaction I felt that night and the importance of recognizing staff achievements. I always made sure other managers recognized fishery officer achievements as well.

I had reasons to celebrate that evening—and I felt like it the next morning. I returned to Quesnel and swaggered with pride as a new father must. January 20 was a fantastic day!

Doing More with Less

Some intellect in Ottawa devised a new slogan for the round of budget cuts we were experiencing—*Doing More with Less*. Budget cuts seemed to always hit the field staff hard, meaning fewer patrols and more impacts on the resource.

The slogan was all the buzz when several hundred staff from all programs gathered for the 1988 All Staff Meeting in May. The evening social gatherings provided an opportunity to meet friends and co-workers from around the region. The daytime meetings were filled with speakers and information sessions.

One senior manager spoke flippantly about the job of fishery officers and referred to them as "state troopers." It's not uncommon for people without an understanding of enforcement to be especially ignorant of the risks and challenges of the job. The fishery officers in the room were upset with his remarks.

It just so happened I had an opportunity to address the entire group of staff the next day when I was called forward to receive an Outstanding Initiative Award. I asked for, and was granted, the microphone for a few words.

I spoke briefly: "I must apologize for being a few minutes late this morning due to a very late evening with friends. I know

I killed more than a few brain cells but that shows Outstanding Initiative because I'll now be doing more with less. If I keep that up I might turn into a supervisor. Oh, and to Mr. Manager who spoke yesterday, not bad for a state trooper, eh?" I held the award up and left the stage to a standing ovation. There were even some managers standing.

I look back at those comments today and realize my direct method of communication may have caused angst for some managers but it sure received strong support from the open-minded managers and all field workers—and I did go on to prove I'd killed enough brain cells to become a manager.

Although those budget cuts were difficult to accept, I learned things could be worse. I happened upon some historical information one day that dealt with enforcement on the Fraser River in the late 1890s. Fishermen on the Fraser River discarded all their fish guts in the river and a keen fishery officer of the time wanted to address the public's concern for the fish waste and enforce the *Fisheries Act*. His reward was a pink slip. It's unlikely anyone would be fired today for simply enforcing the law; however fishery officer numbers are being reduced, resulting in the same challenges of too few officers to reasonably enforce the act.

Helping Lillooet Officers

Fishery officers gathered in Lillooet early each summer to assist the officers on river patrols. In the Interior, salmon arrived there first and there were usually total closures on the early runs. The number of illegal nets seized was always high.

I went on a jet patrol with Tim Cody a few times and always had fun, especially when people tried to run. Tim and I rounded a curve in the Fraser River on a patrol one day to see six guys running up the bank, one carrying a dip net. Tim quickly nosed the jet boat into the rocks on the beach and I bailed off in high gear.

It was a steep and unstable climb up the rocky bank but I threw my life jacket off and scrambled up as fast as possible with my eyes set on the man with the dip net. I passed the first few guys near the top of the bank before reaching the railroad tracks.

I could still see the guy with the net about a hundred yards ahead. I caught up with the surprised poacher in about two hundred yards and he collapsed on the tracks in a gasping heap. He was fairly co-operative, as most out-of-breath people are, and I walked him back to the jet boat and a chuckling Tim, who was shaking his head at my catch. I was grinning like a Labrador retriever with his first duck.

Here I am, patrolling the Fraser River by jet boat near Lillooet, ready to chase down any rare daytime poachers.

The poacher turned out to be a very dangerous criminal from Prince George. He had a lengthy record of assault on police officers, along with a multitude of serious criminal convictions. The majority of poachers I've encountered have criminal records, many for serious crimes. I caught hundreds of poachers throughout my career, many by running them down on foot, and I never had a single person offer physical resistance as long as I let them run until they stopped. I had learned the best tools of the trade were not the handcuffs, pepper spray or handgun: your words and physical fitness were the most effective weapons.

I patrolled by vehicle with Tim one late evening in the Boston Bar area. Tim was a very quiet person with an incredible physique. His dedication to weightlifting over many years had resulted in arms the size of most legs. He had to have his shirtsleeves tailored to fit his monstrous arms.

Anyway, we were driving along beside the Fraser River and noticed a truck we'd been watching for. Tim did a quick U-turn and pulled the truck over. He approached the driver's door and I went around to the passenger side of the beat-up crew cab.

The river was closed and they had fish in the truck. We ordered the four men out of the truck and asked them to stand on the shoulder of the road while we searched the cab. I found some drugs and weapons in the truck under the seat and I was turning around to show Tim when I overheard one of the four say, "Hey there's only two of them and four of us. Let's beat the shit out of them!"

All I could think of was turning my flashlight onto Tim's massive folded arms. Tim had an evil grin on his face but didn't say a word—sort of like a Doberman waiting for you to run. The same poacher who had challenged his friends looked at Tim's arms and said, "Well, maybe not." I'm quite sure Tim would have handled three of them easily and the fourth would have tried to run away, leaving one for me to catch. You might say they were inTIMidated.

The Eleventh Commandment

Franz and I were on a jet boat patrol near Quesnel checking sites for fishing activity when we encountered a rare sight: two poachers camped on the riverbank in a tent. They were set up beside a large dip stand and had two dip nets, a large fish pit with jugs full of ice, camping gear and so on.

It's not illegal to camp on the riverbank and the two were wise enough not to claim any of the fishing gear. They weren't all that wise though because they said they only had the tent. We advised them we'd take everything but the tent and told them if the owners of the rest of the gear came along they should contact us to get it back.

The two long-faced "wannabe" poachers watched as we loaded everything, including their beer, into our boat. We returned to the site at 3 a.m. to find the two men still camped in their tent busily swatting mosquitoes.

Our patrol continued to an area we didn't cover often because we generally encountered other poachers before we reached it. On this night we arrived to find a large dip stand and a net stashed in the trees. We knew these were poachers but couldn't get back for a few days and decided to destroy the stand and take the net. Before we left I took a large piece of cardboard and wrote "The Eleventh Commandment: Thou Shalt Not Dip Salmon From the Fraser River." It was signed "God."

I only wish I could have seen their faces when they arrived for an evening's fishing and found the sign. Our truck patrol several days later proved these poachers had a sense of humour because they'd turned our sign over and written on the back of it, "Dear God, Get your muffler fixed. We heard you coming." We surmised they must have been spooked by another truckload of poachers because we hadn't been in the area.

One Expensive Sockeye

It was another rainy evening of patrolling with the boys from Vancouver. I was in a vehicle with Robert, and Franz was with Ian. Franz and Ian headed north of town to check sites while Robert and I headed south. We caught a couple of poachers without any problems or issues.

Franz and Ian called around 3 a.m. saying they needed some help. They were fine but wanted us to get there as quickly as possible with a tow truck. It took an hour to reach them on a twisty, slippery trail down to the river, where they told us a remarkable story.

The officers had parked over a mile from the river to ensure the poachers didn't see their lights coming down the road. They knew someone was at the river by the fresh tracks in the mud. They parked their vehicle, donned their rain gear and started the slippery walk down the hill.

They were halfway to the river when they saw headlights coming up from the river. The poachers had decided to leave and the officers were a half mile from their truck, so they stood at the side of the road and waited for the truck to arrive. They stepped onto the road as the slow-moving truck came to within a hundred yards of them, but the occupants of the truck had no intention of stopping and the driver floored the accelerator when the officers shone their lights on them. The truck came fishtailing down the road as the officers dove out of the way. One officer threw his flashlight into the air as he dove into the ditch and it hit the centre of the windshield, which shattered before the light bounced into the ditch.

The officers climbed back onto the road and watched the tail-lights of the truck as it sped away but the driver lost control as he approached a narrow section of the trail and his left front tire struck a large boulder. The truck veered right and hit a rock bluff before swerving left, off the trail and down a twenty-foot drop, rolling before it came to a stop.

The officers ran to the truck to find two men, one lying on the ground unconscious and the other sitting behind the wheel in a dazed, confused state. The officers quickly attended to the unconscious poacher, who came round and appeared to be okay except for a few cuts he'd received from being thrown from the truck.

The officers looked in the pickup to find a net and one lonely sockeye. Fishing had been poor and the poachers were leaving early. The two admitted poaching, as they staggered around surveying their totally destroyed truck, a brand new Ford four-by-four. The two were co-owners of a local logging company and certainly didn't need to poach for food; it was just the Cariboo tradition.

The truck was hauled out and the two men were taken back to town. The courts dealt with them with large fines and forfeiture of their gear but their fishing costs were far from over.

I knew that insurance was void if someone had an accident while committing a criminal activity so I called the local ICBC (Insurance Corporation of British Columbia) and talked to an insurance specialist there. He told me that poaching would qualify as criminal activity and that ICBC were very happy to receive the information. The truck, worth about $15,000 at the time, was a total write-off and the insurance was void. This was certainly the most expensive sockeye ever!

Poacher with a Pistol

I was asleep at home one hot August night, which was unusual because I worked almost every night during the summer. As it turned out, this night would be no exception. The phone rang at around 3 a.m. A First Nations fisherman was reporting some poachers on the local reserve.

I decided to check the site out before calling anyone else in case the poachers had already left. I felt safe climbing down the secret trail overlooking the site. I crawled to the bank's edge to find five people. Although it was dark I recognized three of the guys, including a poacher I'd caught twice the same summer, making this his third offence in two months.

I was close enough to hear their conversation, finding it quite entertaining when they talked about Casper the fishery officer. I planned on returning to my truck and calling for help when I heard one of the group say, "If a guy wanted to kill someone now, Larry here could just pull his gun out, shoot him and throw him in the river. It's that easy, heh?"

It was shocking to hear those cold, deadly words, and I started shaking as the reality of chasing poachers once again struck me. I crawled back to my trail, returned to the truck and called the

RCMP for support. They were all busy at a serious domestic dispute and no one was available so I called the local conservation officer and his large German shepherd partner. They arrived in twenty minutes, but in the meantime I went back down the trail and followed the main trail to find the poachers' vehicle, an old truck, parked at the trailhead with a few fish in the back. I looked in the truck and found the registration papers showing the owner was Larry. I searched the cab and found a loaded handgun in a shoulder holster stuffed under the driver's seat. Could this be Larry's gun or did they have another one at the river?

I took the gun and holster back to my truck and joined the C/O and his canine companion. We hiked into the fishing site to find everyone still fishing. The best way to get someone's attention in the dark is to identify yourself and let the dog bark. The universal language of German shepherds froze them in their tracks.

We called them up the bank one at a time to deal with them, including searching them for weapons. We called Larry's name first and the bewildered poacher came up the trail. He complied, put his hands on his head and submitted to the search by the C/O supervised by the dog.

We didn't find any weapons at the site. The group co-operated for the most part, except for Moe. Moe's third offence in three weeks would mean some jail time and he knew it. He was charged for the additional criminal offences of uttering threats and obstruction.

The sun was rising when we walked back to the poacher's truck. Larry walked to the driver's door of his pickup, opened the door and reached under the seat. He jumped up and said, "Where is it? You can't take that!" proving our suspicions that Larry's IQ was near that of the fish in his truck.

Larry was "under-witted" by his fishing partner Moe, whom we caught three nights later for the third time in six days and his partner Curly for the fifth time. Moe was put in jail to appear before a judge the following morning. The unimpressed judge gave Moe twenty-four days in jail for his first two offences and trial dates were set for the rest.

I encountered poor Moe shortly after he was released from jail. He was on the riverbank with a group of people I was observing but he didn't try fishing despite encouragement from his friends. At one point Poacher Moe yelled out, "Hey, Randy, are you sneaking up on us?"

Moe eventually couldn't resist the lure of salmon poaching, and on August 16, 1989, we caught him for the sixth time in twenty-five months. The judge released him with a 10 p.m. to 7 a.m. curfew and he was ordered not to be within a half mile of any fishing site and not to handle any Native-caught fish.

One of Poacher Moe's friends was charged for impaired driving. Bill the Brain had illegal salmon in his trunk despite having been caught poaching three times. The RCMP were pleased to see him charged again because they knew we were receiving larger fines for poaching than for impaired driving. His eventual trial netted him another three months in jail.

Under the Cottonwood Tree

A large, lonely cottonwood tree stood over one of the most active fishing sites in the area, located on the Quesnel Reserve. We'd catch people fishing illegally over and over again at this location using the same technique.

I'd don my camouflage coveralls, take a hidden trail through the trees and crawl across the open grassy field on my belly until I reached the cottonwood tree. I'd lie there watching and listening until I had enough evidence, then call for my partner to drive in and park next to the tree. I'd jump up, pull off my coveralls, throw them in the vehicle and act like I'd just exited the vehicle. It worked every time.

One summer evening I was by the tree watching a group of seven or eight people actively fishing. It looked like a poacher's reunion of people I'd caught over the past few years. I listened to the entertainment for quite a while.

"I wonder where Randy is tonight?" one wondered. One replied, "Yeah, he's probably watching us right now." It was so tempting to answer and I almost burst out laughing. One of them stood up, picked up a six-foot-long two-by-four and started swinging it like a baseball bat while looking out across the river: "Come on

Randy, I'll drive you home." They all laughed and someone said I must have some new scope to watch them so closely. "Yes, but how does he know what we talk about too? He must have our campfire bugged." I'm glad they were laughing loudly because I could hardly contain myself.

I let them carry on until I'd seen them all fish and then I called Franz. He drove in and I followed the routine once again. I approached the group and they all denied fishing. I told them who fished, what order they fished in and how many each of them had caught before stopping. They looked at each other in despair.

One guy erupted into a rage and profanity spree, threatening to get me but four of the others in the group restrained him. I was relieved to have their assistance given that there were a total of fifteen people at the site. I dealt with the seven who had actively fished and left them all still wondering.

Charging the Ministry of Forests

I was patrolling the Swift River system in the spring of 1989 and encountered a large logging operation near the river. The loggers were cutting cottonwood trees on the snow-covered flats where a maze of small channels lay hidden under the snow. I knew the area was valuable coho fry habitat and a large area of it had been destroyed. I didn't remember seeing any logging applications for this site.

I started by taking a series of photographs and then taking statements from all the loggers at the site. I returned to Quesnel late that night and called for some help to visit the area on the following day.

The next morning I visited the Ministry of Forests office and met the forester responsible for the area. He brought the file to the meeting and I glanced through the hundred pages, which gave authority to the logging company among other pertinent information. I was scanning quickly until I saw my name handwritten on a page. The note said, "There are serious environmental concerns with this logging. I suggest you call Randy Nelson of Fisheries and Oceans."

I tried not show any surprise and kept scanning through the file.

I asked if I could copy some pages for the investigation. The forester took me to the copier and I handed him a number of pages that he copied and handed back to me. When I handed him the one with my name on it he turned white before saying, "I don't think I can give you any more right now." I said, "That's okay, I can get them later. These are very helpful." Helpful was an understatement; this was a smoking gun. I'd learned that the senior manager had probably read the comments and ordered the staff to not contact me.

I asked if I could meet with the manager. I knew the guy from his previous job with a large logging company. I had had issues with some of his company's logging practices and had a good idea he would approve logging without regard for fish or wildlife values.

The manager was very nervous during my interview. He blamed the logging company for the mess but did not want to have his staff assist me any further. I had to remind him of the *Fisheries Act* powers before he relented and had some of his staff provide statements. I knew and trusted a couple of staff I interviewed but they were cautious about their answers for fear of retaliation from the manager.

Swift River, 1989—Surveying the damage and garbage left behind by an inconsiderate logging operation.

Swift River, 1989—Checking the small side channels teeming with coho fry under logging debris. The Ministry of Forests had approved the logging despite being warned of potential damage by their own staff.

I worked over the next few months to gather more information. I set fry traps in the side channels to catch fish and prove the area was fish habitat. I had a meeting in Vancouver with senior staff to discuss the case and consider the possibility of charging the province. The evidence was solid, although nothing pointed to one responsible party and the decision would be to charge them all if charges were laid.

A search warrant was prepared and executed on the Ministry of Forests office. I knew where the file was and went straight to it with the warrant. I also seized several file boxes of other pertinent evidence from the offices.

Charges were eventually laid and a trial date was set. I met with the prosecutor the evening before the trial in Quesnel. At 8 p.m. the phone rang and the lawyer had a brief conversation. He hung up the phone and told me someone from Ottawa had called and the charges were being stayed. We were both shocked, as the direction came without explanation or reasons. I later found out a senior bureaucrat in Ottawa had contacted a senior provincial bureaucrat long before the trial was set. It may have been just a very curious coincidence—not.

The Ministry of Forests immediately started working with other agencies, including DFO, to develop the Forestry Practices Code; another curious coincidence. I strongly believe it was part of the agreement between the federal and provincial governments in exchange for dropping the charges. The code could have become a useful document if it had ever been properly enforced.

The staying of charges was another devastating example of how high-level politics can invade the judicial system. I was learning that many decision makers have no idea how much their decisions can negatively impact the resource, not to mention the morale of staff.

I started to look at other employment opportunities, such as the Canadian Wildlife Service. Environment Canada contacted me about two separate jobs, suggesting I apply for the position of senior investigator with them and also requesting I apply for a senior position in Ottawa. I went through all three processes successfully and considered my options.

I came to the realization that politics is everywhere and that I truly enjoyed the work I was doing. I decided to try to influence more decisions within the organization. I wasn't afraid to speak out and management knew that. I promised myself not to allow political interference in legal matters without a fight.

The reality of the staying of charges had not set in when, in mid-January 1991, the Gulf War started. It was another reminder that no matter what negative experiences one might encounter, there are almost always worse events that put your own in perspective.

Road Blocks

DFO officers used to participate in multi-agency road checks on major highways. Enforcement staff from every agency in the country would converge on the Trans-Canada Highway at Rogers Pass or Jasper Park on Highway 16. The checks would go on around the clock for several days.

A vehicle travelling to Alberta was checked near Jasper and found to have several large Chinook salmon. The driver admitted he'd purchased the fish from a Native the day before. That alone wasn't that interesting but this guy's criminal record was astounding.

The driver was forty-two years old and had been in prison for all but fourteen years of his life. He had more scars on his face than the Precambrian Shield and tattoos to match. The guy co-operated but was more nervous than a cat at the dog pound. I thought he might be a drug user and be having some withdrawal symptoms. Finally he asked me if he could get his cigarettes from the glovebox in his car.

I retrieved his cigarettes and handed the two packs to him after checking to make sure they were real. The odd thing was he never lit one up. He quickly tucked a packet under each sleeve of his T-shirt while nervously glancing around. He calmed right down once he had the cigarettes. I later learned that cigarettes are the currency in prison and he'd been in prison so long he couldn't bear the thought of someone stealing them.

Another check was on a very chatty male driver. He proceeded to tell us he'd been an RCMP officer for thirty-two years and was currently a professional photographer for a national conservation organization. He had four times his limit of coho salmon in the truck; so much for conservation.

Two Alberta men went through with forty-two coho. The fish were not on ice and most had not even been cleaned. The fish had spoiled and smelled horrible. It's one thing to take so many fish but even worse if they have to be thrown away.

A motorhome with two elderly men drove up one afternoon and I asked the usual questions about drugs, firearms and alcohol. I asked whether they had any fish and the response was no. Then I heard a child's voice from the back of the motorhome say, "Yes we do, Grandpa!"

Grandpa had a case of "convenient Alzheimer's" and forgot about the six sockeye he'd purchased from a Native in Kamloops. I talked to him and the young boy at length and tried to make sure that Grandpa wouldn't be critical of the boy when they drove away.

An attractive female officer attended a road check in Jasper one fall. Two young Albertans were checked and had some minor fisheries offences. I stood by as the officer professionally handled the case, writing them both a ticket and seizing their fish. The two young men stood quietly until she was done. Then one blurted out, "Thank you! Thank you! You are the most beautiful thing I've ever seen write a ticket!" The officer could only smile as the two happy men drove away.

One of the park wardens attending a road check in Jasper was seven feet tall. He had a well-proportioned physique and didn't look tall from a distance until he stood beside someone else. A truck driver had stopped at the check when the seven-foot warden walked up to the side of the truck to chat with the driver. The warden was chatting through the truck window when the driver suddenly leaned out the window and looked down, "Oh my God, you're not standing on my running boards, you're standing on the ground!"

A check in Rogers Pass was run during the construction phase of the Mount Macdonald train tunnel, and rock-tunnelling crews went through the checks every day. All of them were understanding of the slight delays each morning and evening, except one particular driver on his way through one morning. An officer leaned down to talk to him and was blown away by the smell of alcohol. The officer wanted to check his alcohol level and had him use the Breathalyzer, where he blew three times the legal limit — at 8 a.m. on his way to work with blasting equipment and rock drillers! A small duffel bag sat on the front seat of the truck and the impaired driver claimed it was his lunch. He was probably right, but his definition of lunch was fourteen Kokanee beers.

I kept track of all the fish we encountered during a two-day road check in Jasper National Park and I estimated that between three and four tons of fish travelled into Alberta over a twenty-four-hour period in the summer. I wonder if some of the "missing sockeye" went there?

The road checks were a great tool for raising public awareness but DFO's involvement ended when a retired judge from Alberta had his salmon checked by a fishery officer and challenged DFO's authority. The legal experts agreed to an out-of-court settlement and ended DFO's participation in these checks. Perhaps some day government will realize the value of the road checks and allow them again.

Assisted by Alien Technology

My fifth summer in Quesnel was somewhat boring compared to the previous four. That was a good thing for the fish. Poaching had lost its popularity through strong media coverage and support in the courts. We had to go farther and look longer to find anyone fishing illegally—much like listening to old fishermen tell stories of how many fish they used to catch.

We headed out one evening to try our new infrared spotlight and scope. The one-million-candlepower light had a red glass cover, allowing only infrared light to pass through it. The scope could see the light but the naked eye couldn't. It almost seemed unfair. The only downfall was the spotlight couldn't be shone directly at people or they might see a hazy red glow if they looked directly at the light.

Franz and I walked a long trail to the river and found two trucks parked at the trailhead. We walked to the riverbank overlooking the fishing site to try our new scope. It took a bit of practice to hold the light while looking through the scope, but when we held it correctly the poachers were easily visible.

We watched long enough to determine four males were fishing and then waited for them to come back to the trucks. Ten minutes later we saw a flashlight climbing up the trail and hid ourselves behind the poachers' trucks. The poachers crested the bank and turned their light off before quietly, slowly walking toward us. They were about ten feet away when we stepped out and identified ourselves.

The four startled poachers dropped the fish and nets and screamed like little girls. They were scared! Nobody was willing to try running and that was a bit disappointing. We quickly dealt with the four co-operative guys before they told us what had happened.

They were fishing and happened to look up in the trees to see a glowing red light hovering above. Uneasy, they decided to leave but the light had appeared to be hovering above the trucks and that's why they were so cautious about approaching their vehicles. We showed them our equipment before they left.

One of the poachers called a few days later to advise me they all intended to plead guilty in court. He also said, "You guys scared the shit out of us! We were sure that red light was a UFO!"

He was right in a way—it was a Uniformed Fishery Officer.

Hook, Line and Sinker

One particular fish seller had become a real pain in the posterior many times over. We caught him with a large amount of salmon during a closed time and really wanted to do something special with him. The creative plan resulted from a few very late nights without much sleep.

The Vancouver officers were helping when we caught Mr. Big for the sixth time in three years. I was interviewing him in our patrol car with him seated in the passenger seat. Ian, the creative thinker who helped plan the trick, was outside the car dealing with the bags of sockeye we'd seized from him.

Ian had a telephone line tester device, about three inches by five inches with a wire protruding from the bottom. There was a red and a green light on the front of the tool. I had placed this in my front shirt pocket before Mr. Big got into the car. Ian had taken an old fuse from a car and carved some of the plastic to make it look like a small electronic chip.

I was asking Mr. Big a series of questions about the fish and he was watching Ian go through the bags of fish very carefully. Ian pulled out a small sockeye and held it up for all to see while looking at it very closely. He placed the sockeye on the hood of the car in front of Mr. Big and walked around to my door. I rolled down the window as Ian asked, "That was a three- or four-pound sockeye, wasn't it Randy?" "Yes Ian, it was one of the smaller ones."

Ian pulled out his knife, rolled up his sleeves and started to carefully slice the sockeye into thin strips just behind the head. Mr. Big's eyes were fixated on the sockeye and he had to ask what was going on. I told him we were looking for something.

Ian then began to open the small slits in the sockeye and feel through the flesh. He was holding the altered fuse in the palm of his hand and slipped it between the folds of the fish without either of us noticing. He then went back through the folds and "found" the fuse. He made a very obvious announcement as he gleefully pulled the fuse from the sockeye, "I think we found one, Randy!"

I had my wristwatch set to beep exactly ten seconds after hitting a button on the side of the watch. Ian came walking around the car and held the fuse out to me. I reached into my shirt pocket for the line tester while touching the button on my watch. I started to count to ten in my head as I took the fuse from Ian. I touched the fuse to the line tester exactly as my watch started to beep. "Yes, that's the one, Ian. Good work!"

Mr. Big slumped down in his seat. "That's not fair. You guys are tracking the fish!" He took the plan hook, line, sinker, bobber and rod! Word spread through the community faster than the internet about fishery officers tracking sockeye to catch lawbreakers.

We worked on more ideas to feed the rumours. Ian made a "satellite receiver" using a large magnet as the base and stand for the satellite dish. The dish was a fourteen-inch stainless steel salad bowl with the centre ring from an angel food cake pan mounted inside. Wires and gadgets were attached to make a very realistic-looking device. That sounds hard to believe but we only used it at night mounted to the roof of our truck while driving through a few strategic locations such as the local reserve and past Mr. Big's house. We'd stop to chat with locals, who were always curious about the device on our truck.

The final tool was made from an old fax machine and it was

mounted in the same patrol truck as the satellite dish. An aerial photo of highlighted poaching sites was placed between the rollers. Ian was interviewing another poor poacher when he said, "Just a minute, I'm getting a picture from the satellite." He reached over to the machine as it fed out the satellite photo to the absolute amazement of the poacher.

This story may sound unbelievable but when you realize this was the early 1990s and the tracking devices were observed by so many witnesses, it was absolutely solid. It also helped that poachers were generally not computer scientists.

A friend of mine worked as an RCMP guard. He told me about a poacher who'd been arrested and placed in cells for not appearing in court. The poacher told him the whole story about the satellite dish, the trackers and the satellite pictures the fishery officers were taking at night, even though he'd never seen them personally. This was undoubtedly the most rewarding and successful prank I'd ever been part of. It no doubt contributed to the drop in poaching throughout the area. As it turned out, our fake technology became a reality, with sophisticated tracking devices available today that can do exactly what we dreamt up twenty years earlier.

BCWF Helps Out

The BC Wildlife Federation usually supported the efforts of fishery officers in BC. I attended a few meetings to meet some of the members. They had a great bumper sticker that read, "Poachers are Thieves! Please Report Them!" I asked for a handful of the stickers before heading back to Quesnel.

I always carried one in my pocket for the rare occasion when we just might not have enough evidence to charge someone. One such event took place on the Quesnel River late at night. We drove along the road into the canyon area where we usually walked in. This night we were being lazy and drove the last mile. We arrived at the canyon and started looking around the large rocks where fishing usually happens.

We found wet rocks and fish blood beside a few large coolers, one of which was filled with various kinds of liquor. We searched around but couldn't find any sign of poachers. It seemed strange that they'd disappeared because we would have seen them climb onto the road. We were just about ready to leave when my flashlight reflected on something on a rock near the river's edge.

I crawled down to the object to find the tip of a dip net sticking out of a small cave in the rocks. I shone the light into the cave to see a man curled up in a ball clutching the handle of the net. I took him back to the coolers.

The guy said he'd just come down to the river to look around. He'd found the dip net but hadn't used it and he didn't know who owned the booze. It was evident to us we'd made a mistake by driving in and spooked the guy. We decided to take the net and coolers, and we told the guy if the owners of the booze and net returned they could come into our office and discuss it.

We took our portable party and net back to the truck. I took one of the "Poachers Are Thieves" stickers and put it on the rear bumper of his truck just before the guy came walking up. When he saw it he said, "Where did that sticker come from?" I said, "I'll bet it's some concerned citizen who doesn't like poaching and is putting them on the vehicles of all the good people who don't poach." He started to speak but stopped. He tried to hide his smile as he climbed into his truck and left.

The Whistler's Demise

Just when I thought I'd seen every method of avoiding getting caught I happened upon a group with a lookout posted above their site. I had crawled into the site and nearly missed seeing the guy sitting in the bushes not ten feet from me.

The lookout was constantly scanning the riverbanks through a pair of binoculars. I quietly watched all three poachers at the river take turns catching sockeye. I then watched the lookout and I was surprised to see he had a referee's whistle on a string around his neck. His plan was evidently to blow the whistle to alert the poachers on the river. It seemed like a fairly good plan.

I waited until the lookout was watching through the binoculars and then slowly moved toward him. It's amazing how close you can get if you move slowly. It took about fifteen minutes before I was right behind the lookout.

I had left Franz in the vehicle waiting for two clicks on the VHF radio before driving in to the site to join me. Now I signalled him to drive in. The headlights of the patrol truck were soon visible and the lookout grabbed the whistle and blew it loud and long. Everyone at the river stopped fishing and sat on the shoreline.

I tapped the lookout on the shoulder. He lifted off the ground like he'd been shot. He turned to face a shiny fishery officer badge and a smiling face. I took his whistle and told him not to say a word. I took him about fifty feet to Franz, who was waiting at the vehicle, before running back to the group on the river.

I climbed down the trail to the three guys sitting sipping their beer. They appeared calm and confident as they were certain I hadn't seen them fishing. They claimed they'd just arrived at the river to have a beer and didn't know anything about the dip net and flopping fish in front of them. I wanted to have some fun and asked, "Did any of you guys hear a whistle?" "No," they replied in unison. "That's strange. I was sure I heard a whistle just like this one," as I pulled the whistle from my pocket and blew on it.

Their smiles slowly disappeared as I proceeded to tell them I'd been watching for over an hour and observed each of them catch salmon. They couldn't help but ask how I'd seen them without their lookout seeing me. I told them they'd have to wait until court to hear the whole story.

Quesnel to Powell River

Lorraine and I were looking for our next adventure—to move somewhere we hadn't been. The opportunity arrived after our fifth summer in Quesnel, when a Powell River position opened. I applied and we were off for a house-hunting trip in the fall of 1990.

We had really enjoyed our years in Quesnel despite some of the difficult events that occurred. We left behind many friends, and a few who were not friends, and headed for the Sunshine Coast.

Our three children were excited about the new adventure but they were all concerned we wouldn't have snow at Christmas. How could the reindeer pull Santa's sleigh if we didn't have snow? It turned out we were in time to see Powell River's first white Christmas in twenty years and Santa made the trip without a hitch.

Powell River hadn't had a fishery officer for some time and that became evident in the first week. I was notified of a spill of about 20,000 gallons of raw effluent from the local pulp mill. When I attended and started asking questions, the manager I met was surprised at my visit. He asked why I'd shown up and I told him, "I've just moved here and I take all environmental problems seriously. I'm here to investigate and collect evidence. If there is adequate evidence the pulp mill could be charged." It was obvious they hadn't been checked in a long while.

I returned to the pulp mill several times to conduct drain tests on their effluent pipes and I learned they had a discharge pipe feeding straight into the ocean. The pipe didn't appear on any of their plans and some of the staff didn't even know it existed. It was just another example of the corporate arrogance shown by so many large companies. The company rerouted the pipeline into a treatment area only because they'd been caught.

I was happy to learn that clam diggers often tried to run away when caught fishing illegally. My first clam patrol occurred on a cold late-November evening in an area called Okeover Inlet. Another officer and I approached a group of nine clam diggers on this night. The area was open for digging so our intention was to check for licences and size limits. Everyone seemed friendly and legal — something I wasn't used to. We'd checked them all but one digger who was farther down the beach.

Just as I approached the lone digger he dropped his rake and sprinted off into the darkness. This would be fun! There was nothing but wide-open beaches around us so I quickly caught up to him and ran behind him, waiting for exhaustion to set in.

The man was running fairly fast when he literally disappeared in front of me. He'd stepped into a small cold creek running through the tidal area. The guy went right under the water before coming up gasping for air. He didn't stop though; he went another fifty feet before falling into another small stream.

This time he crawled out of the water and collapsed on the beach. The cold wind combined with the frigid water meant hypothermia would quickly set in. I took the shivering man back to the truck where my partner stood laughing out loud. We put the shivering man in our warm truck to deal with him before taking him back to his residence.

The very next night we patrolled some more clam beaches at night and came to a remote contaminated beach that no one should be digging on. The beach was over a hundred yards wide and about a mile and a half long. We followed some footprints with our flashlights and they led us to a lone male digging. After raising his rake above his head and yelling at us he too started sprinting. "Yahoo!" I yelled and took off after him into the darkness, waiting for him to drop, but this chase was different from most; this guy could run. I had to run flat out for half a mile before I closed the gap and he finally stopped. He threw down his rake, dropped to his knees and wheezed, "I can't believe you caught me!"

I handcuffed the man and walked him back to my partner. He turned out to be a commercial digger; his clams would be sold in stores and restaurants. Digging clams on contaminated beaches for commercial sale is extremely dangerous to the public, and the courts would treat him with severity.

This digger became my best informant in the area for reporting illegal clam digging but I didn't have many more chases with diggers as word spread about the officer who was running down poachers.

Our stay in Powell River was shortened when I was asked to work in New Westminster for a while. After a few months I won a competition for a position in Kamloops and my understanding family loaded up once again for yet another move.

Kamloops

The move to Kamloops opened up many opportunities for our family. Kamloops is a very vibrant, sports-minded city with a great climate. The work opened up new challenges with poachers, polluters and politics.

Illegal sales of salmon in the interior always presented significant challenges. The first challenge was to convince managers in coastal areas of the issue. In the ever-competing world of resources most coastal DFO staff know few of the issues in the Interior. The reality is that both regions have their own particular problems.

DFO managers have always insisted that officers must obtain coastal experience to develop their careers. No one (except me) suggested they should also acquire Interior experience and the bias among managers has always been in favour of the coast; that is, until a new inquiry pointed out the gap.

I conducted a random survey of restaurants and stores selling fish and questioned them on the number of times businesses were approached to purchase illegal fish. I surveyed over sixty Interior businesses and altogether they admitted to having been approached eighty times by persons selling fish illegally in the previous two months. Some, of course, may not have admitted to being approached, so the real figure could have been much higher.

The survey provided proof of the need to spend some time on the issue. Evidence and patrols quickly resulted in a number of significant charges, and a well-known seller living in Enderby was the first target. "Mr. Crook" was tracked for a week before an arrest was made on Main Street in Enderby one summer afternoon.

His van and fish were seized before officers followed the trail of sales he'd made the previous week, a trail that led through a number of Interior cities with some very entertaining results.

A budgie ranch near Vernon was one of the locations we visited with a search warrant. The man admitted to the purchase and his fifty sockeye were seized. The congenial rancher gave us a guided tour of his massive budgie spread as thousands of the birds drowned out our conversation. I thought they were noisy until I met his wife. Few people have heard language as colourful as hers was, as she watched her husband's van being towed away.

Fish versus "Progress"

I moved into a supervisor position in Kamloops, which meant less patrol time and fewer investigations. I'd known that would happen going into the job and I felt ready to take on the challenges of a supervisor. I knew that support for the department was paramount but I vowed to hold the fishery officers accountable and support them whenever possible. I strove for a balance, feeling that too many staff forgot where they'd come from when they moved into management.

My first few months in 1992 were busy. In mid-September a call came from Lillooet and I had to drive over to check it out. I took the habitat biologist with me to check the report of a major habitat destruction incident on the Bridge River. We arrived to find the biggest habitat destruction case either of us had ever seen. BC Hydro was operating a series of major dams on some river systems in the area and had opened a discharge gate, resulting in the scouring out of over twenty miles of fish habitat.

The magnitude of the damage showed the remarkable power of water. D-8 Cats working for weeks could not have caused as much havoc as this single incident. I was asked to lead the investigation due to my experience in large habitat files.

BC Hydro hadn't promptly notified DFO or the public about the sudden release of water. If anyone had been near the stream's edge they could have been washed away by the rolling wall of water, rocks, mud and trees scouring its way to the Fraser River. We will never know how many fish were destroyed in the action.

I conducted numerous interviews, took pictures and arranged for search warrants over the next few months to try to piece together the reason for their actions.

I was amazed at the corporate arrogance and lack of co-operation they displayed over the course of my work. BC Hydro staff provided virtually no assistance during the search of their offices, but I understood them wanting to avoid being charged and convicted, and I accepted their lack of support.

I stood beside a long row of file cabinets as the manager read the search warrant before leaving me standing in the large open office. I glanced along a row and noticed the letters *DFO* on one cabinet in the middle. "I guess I'll start here," I said as the manager walked away. Boxes of files, memos and information were taken away for reviewing.

The next day a senior BC Hydro manager went on a media damage control mission, declaring that if the fishery officers had come to them and asked for the information, it would have been given to them. I called his bluff by phoning him the next day and asking if that offer still stood. He stammered before saying, "Yes." I provided them a list of items I was interested in receiving; some of these were eventually provided.

I needed to prove the company had failed to perform due diligence before opening the spillway. There was ample evidence that proved major habitat damage but we had to prove they could have taken other measures to avoid the major release of water. I took over a hundred written pages of statements from BC Hydro staff, reviewed thousands of pages of documents and pieced together seventy rolls of film taken from flights over the river.

BC Hydro had a manager whom I'd call a self-proclaimed PR specialist. He oozed niceness just like Fred Rogers in the old

TV show *Mr. Rogers' Neighborhood*. This Mr. Rogers managed to convince a few of the more naive DFO staff he was wonderful and that he would help us in any way he could. He held public meetings in the Lillooet community and worked his tail off to convince everyone they were squeaky clean. I finally took him aside at one meeting and told him I thought his message was evasive and misleading. He proved I was correct when I took a statement from him. He suddenly stopped visiting DFO staff after that.

I learned that the water from the reservoir system under investigation was some of the most valuable water in the world. The water generated power three times through a sequence of dams and extreme elevation drops before reaching the Fraser River. This explained why as a matter of principle they keep the dams as full as possible heading into the summer months and avoid releasing water unless it threatens to overtop the dams. In this case they claimed that extreme weather events in Whistler had resulted in unusually high water flows that had compromised their dams and required a sudden release.

Less than a year after the first incident, BC Hydro actions resulted in another major fish kill and habitat destruction, just to prove to me the first wasn't a fluke. Many more months of gathering information from unwilling corporate employees followed.

BC Hydro hired one of the most renowned defence lawyers in the province and the lawyer successfully argued the case over a scheduled five-week preliminary trial followed by an eight-week trial held six years after the event. One of his key arguments was that the extreme weather experienced in Whistler that fall had caused the increased flows. It sounded good except the weather patterns in Whistler were in a different watershed and our lawyer decided not to provide any counter-arguments on that point. Defence also suggested that DFO should have spoken out against the dam in 1948, and the fact that they didn't meant they should be held partly responsible for the reduced fish runs.

I had located some information about the power dam approvals during an extensive search of DFO records in the national archives.

It appears the DFO employee who approved the dam (in the 1940s) thought it would be built twenty miles upstream of the actual site. The mistake came to light only after the approval was given and no one was willing to go back and change it. Unfortunately I found this evidence too late in the investigation.

Regardless of the facts in the case, I felt the judge made the correct decision based on the evidence he was given and acquitted them. If BC Hydro had shown more co-operation and worked with DFO, it could have avoided the lengthy and costly trials. The case did result in some improved procedures and guidelines to avoid a similar spill in the future.

I acknowledge that BC Hydro's task of predicting snow pack and precipitation levels can be difficult and that spills may happen. Hopefully they have learned from the events and will continue to work hard with all agencies to prevent such disasters in the future. It's encouraging to see that no major spills have occurred since those in 1991 and 1992.

One single example of their co-operation was at a facility near Lillooet on the Seton River. Another fish kill had resulted from a spill in that smaller facility, which had a series of five siphons each capable of siphoning 700 gallons of water over the dam every second. The problem was that increases and decreases of 700 gallons per second as siphons were opened and closed were too quick for fish to avoid being trapped or washed away.

They claimed they could only allow changes in water flow in 700 gallon-per-second increments. That sounded reasonable until I asked if they could open one siphon, then slowly close it down while opening the next and so on until the flows were all at maximum. The engineering wizards looked at each other as if I'd just invented the wheel. "Yes, we could do that!" It was an example of how little thought they'd given to changing their procedures to lessen impacts on fish.

The investigation certainly gave me an inside view of BC Hydro that few have seen. It was discouraging and quite disturbing to read what goes on out of public view. They weren't alone in their actions; I've seen the same kind of thing happen in other large companies.

For example, I found a document in the national archives dated September 8, 1960. It was a speech prepared for the opening announcement of the Bridge River hydroelectric facility operated by BC Electric.

The announcement discusses power rates in BC and the engineering feat of harnessing the river. The announcement mentions three factors that determine the cost of hydro power production: type of river; length/terrain of transmission lines; and regularity of river flow. It then goes on to say, "The Fraser is the only large river in our area that meets all three of these low cost conditions, but, unfortunately, the salmon spawning problem prevents you from getting the cheap power it would provide."

This statement is a harsh reminder of where we were and why our fish and wildlife resources were so often on the back burner. They actually had the audacity to publicly announce that salmon were a problem preventing the production of cheaper power.

We have made some progress since 1960 but the lack of movement in properly addressing recommendations from the recent Cohen Commission of Inquiry are a reminder of how low a priority our leadership gives to salmon today.

The Seton dam facility has taken some steps to lessen impact in peak migrations but I believe some sockeye smolts still enter the turbines each spring. If this were to happen in the Lower Mainland, the media would probably pounce.

A lack of media attention to stories outside the Lower Mainland also limits the exposure of some serious environmental stories. It's not that the media aren't interested in the stories—they just can't afford to cover them.

I witnessed the same lack of interest in remote areas within the DFO. I heard a senior manager suggest we shouldn't be spending time on habitat cases in areas where no one would see them; we should put our resources into areas such as Vancouver that were on public view. I thought it was a joke until they scowled at my laughter.

Even today I see public willingness to spend hundreds of thousands of dollars to restore a few of the salmon streams in Vancouver that have been destroyed and diverted into storm sewers and drains over the past century. I support those valiant efforts but I think more can be done to avoid the massive destruction of existing fish habitats outside the Lower Mainland .

I took a helicopter flight throughout the Yukon in 2010 to inspect a series of DFO field camps. We flew over some of the most pristine country on the planet but we also flew over some of the most destructive mining operations imaginable.

Gold mining in the Yukon is destroying hundreds of miles of fish streams as this industry continues to mine gold from stream beds, permanently altering the streams and rendering them unrecognizable.

The Minister of Fisheries (under one federal government) agreed to address the problem years ago by assigning four new fishery officers to work on placer mining problems in the Yukon. The announcement was never followed through and today staff numbers in the Yukon are being scaled back (under another federal government). Both main federal governments in power over the years have ordered reductions in environmental protection officers. Public pressure is vital to ensure everyone is held accountable.

The modern DFO approach to habitat relies on operating guidelines and the expectation that companies will follow those guidelines through "self-enforcement." I view self-enforcement as about as likely to succeed as self-intercourse. It sounds good if you say it fast but it will not work. The bottom line is, money talks and fish don't.

Getting Stabbed

January 31, 1992, was a normal day in the office during the
newly announced budget cuts. I went home and picked up
Darren and Janna, aged four and six, and headed to downtown
Kamloops for a sports card show. We were enjoying our walk
down the street when a man came running around the corner of a
building.

A tall young man chasing him yelled, "Stop him! He stole a
purse!" I grabbed the small, slightly built man with a purse under
his arm and put him to the ground. I recognized the man chasing
him as an employee at the Plaza Bar. I also knew this guy on the
ground might think he was in for some back-alley justice so I said,
"I'm an auxiliary with the RCMP!" The guy threw the purse on the
ground and said, "You've got the purse. Now let me go!" "Well, it
doesn't quite work that way," I said as I helped him to his feet.

The man took off running again. I told the Plaza employee
to stay with my kids while I ran the guy down. I didn't follow my
normal protocol for chases and caught him in about thirty yards.
The man placed his hands on the cement wall of the building
beside us and assumed the search position.

I turned to look for my kids, who were walking toward us with the Plaza employee. I never saw what happened next because I was facing my kids. The Plaza employee later told me the man pulled a knife from his right front pocket, spun around, grabbed me by the collar and pulled me toward him while plunging the knife into my chest. It happened so fast he couldn't even warn me.

The impact of the knife nearly knocked the wind out of me as I staggered back and faced the man. The Plaza employee yelled, "Look out! He's got a knife!" I thought I'd been punched in the chest because I only felt winded and didn't feel any pain.

The stabber turned and ran toward my two kids. It was one of the most helpless, scary moments of my life seeing a crazy guy, obviously on drugs and alcohol, running toward my children with a knife in his hand. There are no words to describe that feeling. Someone was taking care of us because the stabber ran past the kids and kept going.

I told the Plaza employee to stay with the kids and call the police while I ran the guy down. I felt safe leaving the kids with someone I knew and I felt safe chasing him because I knew I could outrun him if he turned on me with the knife. I still didn't know I'd been stabbed. I intended to chase the guy until he dropped.

He ran about four blocks, stopping when he was tired and each time turning to face me with his knife and slashing it wildly through the air, once yelling, "Come on, pig! I'll kill you!" I stayed at least twenty-five feet behind him in case he came at me. The stabber ran across the street in front of the screeching tires of a taxi. "Too bad his brakes worked!" I thought.

The chase ended when he ran through the front door of the Plaza Pub. I yelled at a waiting cab to call the police. I didn't know the guy with my kids had already called the police and reported a stabbing or that the police were combing the streets and back alleys several blocks away looking for a stabbing victim. I approached the front door of the pub and peered in through the small window.

The pub was known as a biker bar and I knew the patrons were more likely to be friends of the stabber than me. I kicked the door open in case he was waiting for me. I opened the door again and poked my head in. I asked a waitress near the door, "Did you see a man run in here with a knife?" She pointed to a man on the floor under a bar table with four people sitting around and said, "You mean him?"

I yelled, "Look out! He's got a knife!" I later realized such a statement raised no concern as most patrons in the pub probably had knives. The stabber crawled out from under the table and ran toward the back of the bar. A large bouncer grabbed the stabber by the shoulder. The stabber took a wild swing at the bouncer's neck with the knife and cut the collar on his shirt. The bouncer didn't know the man had a knife when he grabbed him.

A bouncer is a friend of everyone in a biker bar—that's the law of the jungle—and the stabber had made a big mistake. He was cornered like a lion in the back of the pub by a circle of large men holding chairs. I was in no mood to approach the stabber and elected to watch. The stabber quickly moved toward the stripper's stage and climbed onto it.

A stripper was dancing during the ruckus and, just like the band on the *Titanic* who showed true professionalism, kept performing despite the obvious distractions. The man ran across the stage and stepped on the jukebox, where he slipped and fell to the floor. I ran around the stage, because I didn't want to interrupt the performance and make the crowd angry with me, and on the other side I found the stabber pinned to the floor. A big biker was lying on top of him while a second mountain man was standing on his long hair. The large, hairy biker was holding a pool cue by the small end. He leaned down to the stabber and held the butt end of the pool cue to his forehead and yelled, "Don't you try a fuckin' thing!"

I knew the stabber still had a knife in his hand under the pile of bodies so I crouched down, pulled his arm out and wrenched the knife from his hand. I stood up holding the knife and realized everyone was standing and watching. The place erupted with clapping and cheering. (I think the stripper was jealous.) It was like a live scene from an action movie. Those that weren't clapping were holding knives, sticks and large flashlights. I was sure glad they didn't know I was an enforcement officer.

I told the bouncer to hold the man until the police arrived and I'd return. I ran back to the Plaza employee and my two kids. Police cars were everywhere when I arrived. They all looked puzzled when I ran up. They'd been told I was stabbed and asked me about it. "No, he just punched me." I replied, still in shock. My kids and I jumped into a police car and returned to the Plaza. The hotel manager took the kids into her office while we went to another room where seven police officers were standing around the stabber seated in a chair in handcuffs.

The stabber gave me a puzzled look, "I thought I stabbed you! You told me you were a pig and I tried to kill you!" Those were the most chilling words I'd ever heard; the hair on my neck tingled as I turned away, still wondering why he was saying he'd stabbed me. He obviously wasn't on the dean's list of any major university—he had admitted his guilt in front of seven police officers.

I left the room and travelled to the office with my kids. The RCMP officer asked me one last time before we entered the detachment, "He says he stabbed you. Did you check?" I opened the zipper on my ski jacket and saw three drops of blood on my T-shirt. "Uh-oh! I guess he did!" I lifted the shirt to see a half-inch cut right in the centre of my chest. I felt my heart start pounding as reality settled in.

I spent some time in the detachment giving a statement before taking my kids home. I knew I had to have my wound checked because stabbings don't have to be large to be deadly. When my kids and I walked in the front door we were met by my waiting wife saying, "Where have you been? We have company and you're two hours late!" I said, "I have to go to the hospital because I've been stabbed." That was the best excuse I've ever had for being late, but luckily I've never had to use it again.

Some friends were visiting us and one of them drove me to the hospital. I had lots of time to think about the event as I waited two hours to see a doctor. A nurse finally took me into the emergency room and sat me on a bed facing two other patients on the opposite side of the room. An elderly lady was lying across from me hooked up to all kinds of equipment. I was feeling neglected until the alarms went off on the old woman's monitors and doctors and nurses came running to her bed.

It was like a scene out of a movie. The lady's heart had stopped and they jump-started her with paddles in a matter of seconds. That was a reality check for me; at least my heart was still ticking. A doctor eventually checked me out, poking and probing at the wound. I felt pain for the first time even though I'd been stabbed three hours earlier. The mind is an incredible thing.

The doctor told me if the knife had been a half-inch lower or a half-inch to either side, I'd be dead. The tip of the knife had hit me squarely on the xiphoid process (the tip of the sternum). If I were as lucky in lotteries as I am in life they'd refuse to sell me tickets.

I went home to play cards for the evening with our friends. I never slept a minute the first night and knew that was normal. I was a member of the DFO critical incident stress peer team and had received training on what to expect. I found it strange that the only pain I'd felt was when the doctor opened the cut. Three nights later I awoke in the middle of the night and felt pain in the cut for the second time. I took the bandage off to look. The wound hadn't opened but the pain felt real.

The stabber was charged with attempted murder and attempted aggravated assault for his knife swing at the bouncer. I attended the courthouse to hear the case. The Crown lawyer advised me he'd told the defence lawyer he'd ask for seven years if his client pleaded guilty and ten to twelve years if the case went to trial. The stabber pleaded guilty and was given seven years.

It was a crazy experience and one that I'd wish on no one. (Well, maybe a couple of people.)

I've thought about the incident many times in the years since, and I am so thankful for all the support I was given by everyone involved, including the RCMP, who handled the case with professionalism and empathy; the lawyers; the judge; the doctors; my friends and colleagues; and especially my family.

Lorraine and I were invited to Government House ten months after the event, where I received an award at BC Police Honours ight from the Lieutenant-Governor of BC. The RCMP paid the costs for Lorraine and me to attend the formal dinner. Many years later I received a BC Police Valorous Service Medal. No one goes through this for a medal but recognition surely helps the recovery. Thanks.

I've received a wall-full of awards over the years but one stands out above all the rest. Pat Chamut, the former regional director general of DFO, sent a personal letter to Lorraine. The letter thanked her for supporting me and recognized the importance of a cohesive family. I'll always cherish that letter as the most important recognition anyone could give. I only wish more managers realized what is really important.

Law Enforcement Olympics

I started running to get in shape and chase poachers but my competitiveness pushed me to a level I hadn't dreamt of. I enjoyed racing, and races became the motivation for all my runs. I didn't know how to train properly and had no access to a coach so I learned largely through trial and error and over-training. I raced in over two hundred long-distance races and won in my age group in most races. I had a personal best of 32:09 for the 10K and up to 2 hours 32 minutes for the marathon. I enjoyed the marathon the most.

I heard about an event called the Law Enforcement Olympics that brought together enforcement officers from all over the world every two years for competition. The games were held during the summer and getting time off was difficult but in 1992 I had holidays approved to travel to Washington, DC, for the games.

The games were the biggest international event outside the real Olympic Games and included many former Olympic athletes. Many countries hired their athletes as police officers so they'd be paid a wage and would be able to train for their sport.

In early August, Lorraine and I travelled to Washington where I had entered the 10K cross-country race, the 10K track and the half-marathon, all to be run within four days. I'd trained hard and felt ready when we landed.

I arrived at the starting line for the hilly cross-country course with about two hundred runners from around the globe. I loved the course because I run hills well but I don't like heat and it was over 32°C with 93 percent relative humidity. I ran the first mile cautiously, trying to adjust to the heat. Then I let my instincts take over and raced through the hills, passing a bunch of runners.

I ran up beside one persistent competitor from the United Arab Emirates. He had a look of horror on his face when I pulled up beside him. "What age? What age?" he wheezed. I thought that to be an odd question but answered him. He seemed relieved as I left him on the next hill. I finished the race in second place, winning a silver medal. I talked to him after the race and learned that officers from the United Arab Emirates received $25,000 US for a gold, $15,000 for a silver and $10,000 for a bronze. He said they used to get a Mercedes for a gold. No wonder he didn't want me to pass; he thought I might have been in his age category.

The ten-kilometre race on the track was the very next day, so there was no time for recovery. I rarely run on the track and really don't enjoy it. The heat was even worse—about 35°C. I saw four runners from South Africa wearing full tracksuits sitting on a bench shivering and I had to ask them what was up. They were cold because they often ran in 45°C weather.

I ran the 10K race dousing myself with two glasses of water every lap. The man handing out the water yelled, "Here come the shower man! Here come the shower man!" every lap. I finished in thirty-three minutes and missed out on gold by half a step. I ran to the side of the track and stumbled on the inner track rail, spraining my ankle badly.

I was extremely disappointed with a silver medal but knew my best race was likely to be the half-marathon. Lorraine helped me limp back to the hotel and ice my ankle. The good news was it didn't swell much, but it hurt like hell. I convinced myself I'd be able to race in two days. I hobbled around the next day but couldn't put much weight on it. I'm a strong believer in the power of the mind and visualized myself running the race and winning.

I arose the morning of the half-marathon and headed to the shuttle bus. The ankle was still very painful but I believed the pain would go away. I arrived at the race and went for a slow one-mile warm-up. Then I hobbled to the start line. I swear my ankle stopped hurting fifty yards into the race. I ran the flat gravel course in 1 hour 13 minutes and won the gold medal.

As I crossed the finish line my ankle instantly started hurting again. I still can't explain it and I wouldn't suggest people follow my example but Scandinavian stubbornness in my genes wouldn't let me miss a race after spending so much money to get there. I

Law Enforcement Olympics, Edmonton, 1990—Winning medals in international enforcement races was almost as much fun as chasing poachers.

watched one of my Middle Eastern friends come in second, realized I'd just cost him $10,000 US and felt good about it. He was a great sport and we shook hands afterward.

Over the years I raced in five international police/fire events, winning eight gold, six silver and two bronze medals. The main event is now called the World Police and Fire Games. I met many wonderful people, including some former Olympians. Everyone traded shirts, hats or pins at the events and Canadian clothing was highly sought after.

I approached a runner from Zimbabwe who was wearing a T-shirt from the Seoul Olympics and asked if he wanted to trade. He said sure, but he'd like shoes. I questioned him further and he showed me his runners, which were worn right through the bottom to expose the outside half of his bare foot. Here was a world-class athlete, faster than any Canadian ever was, and he couldn't afford shoes. The problem was he wore size nine and I had size thirteen.

I took his name and address home with me. I told fellow runners about it and several came up with a pair of used shoes to send him. The runner had told me he might not get them because their postal workers often stole things they wanted. I thought that was what had happened until I received a letter from him over a year later. In it he wrote, "Thank you so much. I am racing in the shoes and winning many races. Thank you so very much my white friend." Another reminder of how much we take things for granted.

High Seas Flight

Fishery officers patrol the Pacific Ocean aboard Canadian Aurora airplanes throughout the year. The flights involve ten- to twelve-hour days of flying over the open ocean searching for vessels of interest. Vessels located by radar are flown over for photographs and identification.

I volunteered for a six-day trip on which we were scheduled to fly due west of Vancouver to Adak, Alaska, at the tip of the Aleutian Islands, and fly missions from there. The first day was uneventful with few vessels spotted. We landed at the rundown US military base of Adak and it was like visiting another planet! I think it's where military people were sent instead of prison.

It rarely gets far below freezing or above 20°C there and it rains three days out of four all year round—sometimes very hard. The island was void of trees except for a group of ten small evergreens planted in the 1940s. They were only ten feet high but were designated a US National Forest Preserve for their historical significance.

I went for a run in the soggy weather when we landed. I travelled out of town, down a gravel road and found a large asbestos dump with drums of unknown crap leaking unknown liquids into the ditch. One barrel was leaking a bright green substance. I later learned the island was rated one of the top ten most polluted locations in the US. All sorts of Second World War materials were buried in the area. The island has since been cleaned up and the base has been closed.

I couldn't imagine spending a couple of years on this island. I was ready to leave in two days. I was walking to the cafeteria the second evening in the pouring rain when a young couple pulled up and offered me a ride, which I gladly accepted. They were in a very good mood. I commented, "I've been here for two days and you are the first people I've seen smiling." The man quickly responded, "That's because we're leaving tomorrow!"

We left Adak on the third day and located a number of legal Japanese fishing vessels. Our patrol had taken us so far over the Pacific that Hawaii was closer than Vancouver, and we landed at the US military base in Pearl Harbor. It seemed rather strange to see eleven Japanese military aircraft parked on the base; how times can change! Lorraine was a bit surprised when I called her from the poolside in Hawaii, and she showed no sympathy for my sunburn. I thought this must be what it's like to be a senator or senior politician. Just kidding!

The trip back to Comox, BC, included reporting a suspicious vessel to US authorities. The Canadian crew were a pleasure to fly with, although the ten hours of looking out a small window did become monotonous.

Black Friday

February 19, 1993, became known as Black Friday for fishery officers. It was the day a long-standing classification grievance was "solved." Fishery officers had long felt their pay level was less than that of others doing similar jobs but the decision on the issue was delayed for years—until a senior manager addressed a group of officers gathered in Vancouver.

The manager yelled, swore and bullied the roomful of shocked officers. The DFO admitted the officers were doing far more than they were paid for but the solution was unexpected. Officers would no longer do habitat or fish management work; that portion of their job would be done by other staff who would get paid more than the officers. The room was filled with more anger than at any protest I'd witnessed. Another manager at the front asked a few of us standing at the back to come sit down. I responded, "No thanks, I don't think the pain would allow me to sit down right now."

The message and the way it was delivered destroyed some good officers. Some left the organization; others continued but never regained their enthusiasm for one of the greatest jobs in government. I found myself in the middle, wanting to do something but knowing I had to wait for the right time.

The decision unfolded with more devastating news for the officers. Most of the new habitat and fish management positions would come from existing fishery officer positions. It certainly was a clear message: "Don't mess with senior managers or you may be eliminated." It was difficult to understand in the 1990s; the actions seemed more suited to a Third World dictatorship. I filed the experience away and tried to continue having some fun.

Several months after the announced changes I was called to Vancouver to receive a Deputy Minister's Commendation for the stabbing incident. After receiving the award I commented, "The incident I was involved in to receive this award was the scariest day of my life—until reorganization came along." I didn't plan on sitting quietly while the organization crumbled.

Another highly destructive event occurred in the National Park Warden Service. Wardens had asked for the right to carry side arms in the national parks due to the dangers they faced. They patiently followed the procedure to Federal Court and were successful in their battle. However, senior parks managers chose to arm only a selected group of wardens (few of the ones involved in the court challenge were armed). Many of those armed were new, inexperienced officers, some of whom didn't really want to be armed. The result has been that armed park wardens may be called from one end of the park to the other because the warden on site is unarmed. This hardly seems safe or efficient. It was a sad display of bureaucratic egos destroying the morale of dedicated wardens.

Under Pressure

I t was refreshing to get back in the field when summer arrived in 1993. A group of officers worked out of Lillooet for the summer to address the widespread poaching and illegal sales problem. We made a few routine arrests early in July and then finally made a good one.

I was working with Barry Zunti and John Ball on July 18 when we located three poachers fishing across the river near Boston Bar on the Fraser River. We observed them through spotting scopes until dark and continued watching through the night with a night scope.

We knew they were probably an infamous group of poachers considered dangerous to anyone in authority. We drove our two patrol vehicles along the two-hour route to the fishing site, where we planned to stop them on the road rather than at the river. We chose a narrow, steep section of road to avoid them driving around us or running away.

At 5:30 a.m. the truck finally came up from the river. I drove in front of it and the other officer quickly pulled in behind it. They were surrounded and not happy. All three men were immediately placed in handcuffs. The truck box contained 150 fresh sockeye packed in commercial-grade flake ice. These fish were the most professionally prepared fish I'd ever seen outside a commercial plant.

A search of the truck and the occupants located a bag of marijuana, a driver without a driver's licence, a stolen decal on the licence plate, a rifle, a baseball bat, four large knives, an axe, a siphoning hose and a garrotting wire (used to strangle people). We seized their truck and everything in it.

We waited over two hours for a tow truck. The three men were all smokers so we gave them their cigarettes and watched them skilfully light up while in handcuffs. They wanted to brew some coffee on their Coleman stove so we removed the stove and pot from the truck. It was most entertaining to watch one man light up the stove and brew the coffee while wearing cuffs and with ZZ Top's "Got Me under Pressure" blaring on his stereo. He was fined $1,000 and lost his truck, fish and weapons. He died in a motorcycle accident several years later while driving impaired.

Fishery Officers Meet DFO Minister

I n the early 1990s the decision to reduce fishery officer numbers was being implemented and officers were either giving up or getting angry. A few of us decided to form the Society of Pacific Region Fishery Officers to try to raise the profile of enforcement in DFO, something that managers rarely had an understanding of or interest in. Many viewed it as a necessary evil or like something stuck on the bottom of your shoe.

I had heard Fisheries Minister Brian Tobin in the media and thought I'd write a letter to him. I wrote a personal, passionate letter from home asking for a meeting with fishery officers. I did not write the letter for the society; this was a personal plea. I knew that the chances of him even seeing the letter were remote but I felt desperate.

The minister was in BC the next week and he held an open-line radio show. Some fishery officer called in and he asked for a meeting with the minister. The minister agreed to meet with a group of twenty-five to thirty officers two weeks later, on November 2, 1994.

If there was ever a recipe on how to get senior government managers excited, this was it. Phone calls to me from Vancouver and Ottawa were non-stop; most were not from happy people and many involved serious profanity. Most chose to try to intimidate me rather than listen and understand our issues. I told all of them we would simply be repeating the messages we'd sent up the food chain in earlier correspondence. That statement probably made them even more fearful as I strongly suspect our concerns and messages had never reached the minister before.

I was told I'd be chairing the meeting with the minister and had to decide which officers would attend. I asked a small group of highly regarded officers to assist with the presentation. It was most difficult to decide who could attend because everyone wanted to be there. I narrowed the number to twenty-five, trying to include representatives from around the region and a cross-section of personalities. I was worried that one bad outburst could ruin the meeting but we had to move on and include as many as possible.

Our small group met in Vancouver for two days prior to the meeting. Everyone came with statistics and detailed evidence to support our concerns. We had a forty-five-minute presentation nearly complete and I was reviewing the draft when someone dropped a document over my shoulder onto the desk in front of me. I didn't turn to see who dropped it and nor do I care to know.

The document consisted of four or five pages of anticipated questions that senior managers felt we might ask, and included the senior managers' responses. Some of the questions were correct but the responses were filled with inaccuracies and fabrications. I guess that someone up the food chain felt we needed some help, and it was refreshing to know someone cared. I reviewed the dropped document and included some additional information in my presentation, complete with supportive facts that would prevent the misinformation from reaching the minister.

Very senior staff from Ottawa continued to call me right up to the time of the meeting with the minister. The desperate attempts to intimidate and harass me were unnerving but I really felt we had only facts and nothing to hide.

On the evening of November 2, twenty-five uniformed fishery

officers and I waited patiently in the room. I asked all officers to speak respectfully and to the point. If I felt someone had said enough I would ask him or her to stop. We waited anxiously until one of the minister's staff entered the room and asked me to come outside.

I followed the minister's staff into the hallway to a waiting Minister Tobin and two senior DFO staff. I walked up to him and extended my hand. Minister Tobin shook it firmly and said, "Randy, thanks for the letter." I responded, "You're welcome." I know I didn't sound too enthusiastic because I had never met him and wasn't sure he'd even seen the letter, but he gripped my hand very firmly, looked in my eyes and said in a louder voice, "No! Thank you for the letter!" I liked this guy.

We walked into the room of officers where I started to present our prepared information. Brian Tobin had all his staff leave the room; he only wanted to hear from the officers. I was five minutes into the presentation when Minister Tobin said, "Randy, that's important information and I'd like a copy of it but we have twenty-five officers here and I really want to know what's going on. Let's just have an open discussion amongst us." The meeting ended three hours later after very open, professional discussions about the state of conservation and protection. It became very evident he was hearing most of the information for the first time despite it having been raised on numerous occasions.

The minister promised the group he'd take action—and he did. The next day one senior manager had a new job. I'd never seen things happen so quickly in government. I was no longer being sworn at by senior managers; some genuinely tried to work with us, while others chose to work against us. The ones working against us didn't do very well.

A few days after the meeting I received a phone call from one of the minister's staff in Ottawa. He said Minister Tobin had read the entire document and had a few questions. I was able to answer these. The caller also advised me the minister wanted me to contact him if anything arose that I felt was important for him to hear. I listened in disbelief as the caller gave me all the minister's contact information and insisted I call any time, day or night. He also asked me to keep the calls confidential.

I hung up the phone, sat back and pinched myself. I was excited and scared at the same time. If any senior managers got word of my direct line to the minister, I was certain my career would be altered at some point. I knew ministers are only around for a few years and I had nearly twenty left before I would retire voluntarily.

Brian Tobin remained in his position for the next two years. I was very careful to call him only for serious matters after having exhausted all internal attempts to fix a problem. If I ended up calling him, the actions he took were almost instant, usually the next day. One example was the planned reduction in budgets for fishery officers to support a catch-monitoring program that was already short of funding. I placed a call. The very next day the money was reinstated and the senior manager responsible was given a new job.

I learned so much about government during those two years. I learned there were some senior managers I could trust and some I couldn't. I learned that everyone has a boss; you just have to find the boss who cares and will listen. If that doesn't work, try the next one up the food chain. I also learned that as long as you collect facts and wait for the right moment to present them you can change government. It was never easy and always risky but it felt much better than carrying on without trying.

I worked for nearly twenty ministers of DFO and only two stood out to me. Ministers Brian Tobin and John Fraser truly cared about the resource and the field staff. Some others may have done but I never experienced it, and I certainly know a few who didn't care at all. That's one thing about working in government: you know your boss is likely to change positions before you.

Kids Know the Answers

T he year 1994 had dismal returns on the Fraser River and the
minister announced a public review of sockeye stocks on the
river. The review was receiving high media coverage throughout
BC and I was asked to attend my daughter's Grade 4 class and talk
about the job of a fishery officer and the "missing salmon."

I knew I couldn't provide my opinion on the public review,
as I would be testifying on that at a later date. I went before the
enthusiastic class and they listened attentively to my description of
the job of a fishery officer. I was trying to explain the intricacies
of managing salmon and the difficulties in determining who could
catch how many fish when I came up with a classroom exercise to
demonstrate my point.

I had the students move the desks back from the middle of the
room. I told them the aisle down the middle was the Fraser River,
the back of the room was the ocean and the front of the room
were the spawning beds in a river. I asked for volunteers and then
placed twenty of them in the ocean at the back of the room. They
were salmon. Four more were designated commercial fishers, two
were sport fishers, one was a First Nations fisher and one was the
spawning ground.

The rules were: no one could run; the commercial fishers would start first and when they touched a salmon, it was caught and had to follow them to the boat; the same applied to the sport fishers but they had to stand on the banks of the river and wait for the fish; the First Nations fisher had to wait farther upstream to catch salmon. Everyone waited in position until I said go.

The melee unfolded as everyone scurried around catching and being caught. After two minutes I told them to stop and return to their desks. I asked the four commercial fishers to stand up. They were all grinning and happy because they caught lots of fish. The two sport fishers had only caught one fish and the First Nations fisher only had one. Not a single fish made it to the spawning grounds. I couldn't believe how realistic the exercise was.

I then asked the class how we could have done the exercise to make sure some fish made it to the spawning grounds. "Let's make some rules," one quickly declared. The ideas came forward in rapid succession. Many of their ideas were already in place but it was amazing to watch the creative minds of nine- and ten-year-olds working together to resolve their differences. I wish I had recorded the session and shown it to all the user groups.

I then suggested we try the exercise again with some rules they'd developed put in place. We did the entire exercise again; everyone got fish but this time some made it to the spawning grounds. I doubt if we'd need reviews or inquiries if all the user groups and DFO could think as openly about solving a problem as a ten-year-old.

Fraser Sockeye Review

T he Honourable John Fraser headed up the Fraser River Sockeye Public Review Board and testimony from all areas of DFO was heard. It was very evident that many in senior positions wanted the review to focus on management and science shortfalls, and that seemed to be the focus of the review until fishery officers were asked to provide information.

Once again the senior managers trembled as fishery officers presented facts and evidence that placed some of the blame on the lack of enforcement funding. Mr. Fraser was shocked to learn the number of officers had been reduced to such low levels. The resulting recommendations called for increased enforcement funding and a director of conservation and protection in charge of all enforcement officers. These were similar to recommendations made in 1982 in the Pearse Commission's report and every other report and inquiry, past or future. Some people may think I'm biased in calling for more enforcement funding, but I'm certainly not alone. I'm reminded again of Mr. Fraser's comment that to say that lack of funding is the reason for reduced enforcement is "an abdication of the government's constitutional responsibility."

A director position was created, although the director still reported to a fish manager, and the Fraser Sockeye Review did lead to the provision of critical funding for increased enforcement, if only for a number of years. This funding allowed fishery officers to address much long-term illegal fishing activity along the Fraser River. The new equipment, vehicles and operating money immediately improved morale and increased the productivity of fishery officers.

Coastal areas were not so lucky because the funding was only for Fraser River sockeye but they do travel through some of the coastal areas and indirect funding did improve enforcement there as well.

There has never been a review, inquiry or commission that could point directly to the cause of reduced salmon stocks or offer solutions. A group of ten-year-old kids was able to come up with a host of ways to reduce impacts on salmon in one classroom exercise but they had the benefit of being impartial and having no vested interest. It's unfortunate that stakeholders, environmental groups and governments can't approach the problem with the openness and optimism of our children.

Focus on the Fraser

In 1995 we focused on improving enforcement and catch monitoring on the Fraser River. I was asked to lead a group of fishery officers on increased patrols in the mid and upper Fraser River, and Lillooet was the main target of our efforts.

Illegal fishing was out of control that summer. We were catching people fishing in closed times like never before. Over a hundred people were charged in the Lillooet area above Boston Bar. There were some tense situations with a few Native fishers as well. Officers had the tires on their trucks slashed and windows broken, and they fielded a number of threats.

I kept thinking about how easily things had turned ugly at Gill Bay, and wanted to avoid a similar incident. One officer suggested approaching the bands to garner their support and to stop outside First Nations from fishing in their area. Many in DFO ridiculed the idea because they felt the First Nations would never agree. But in the end the First Nations not only banned outside fishers; they also imposed a restriction and banned nighttime fishing throughout the area.

This major breakthrough prevented the majority of illegal fishers from fishing in the area. Nighttime patrols were much easier because anyone encountered was unauthorized and the bands supported DFO's efforts.

Seized fish were often trucked to Vancouver and sold but a change in policy was required to accommodate another new idea. fishery officers wanted to give the fish to needy elders in the community rather than selling them commercially. All the bands welcomed this change. I'll never forget the media coverage showing elders hugging fishery officers. We were making major changes that benefited everyone. It wasn't all easy but it was a positive start and a move to more peaceful, well-managed fisheries.

The regional director general, Paul Sprout, took time out of his personal holidays to stop in Lillooet one evening and experience a night patrol with fishery officers. I worked with him through the night as he experienced verbal abuse, threats from weapons, a sleepless night and the uncertainties that families experience while officers are working at night. It's too bad more managers wouldn't take the time to be enlightened about the work of fishery officers.

The increased patrols certainly reduced the illegal fishing. However, those caught fishing were often dangerous criminals willing to fish regardless of consequences. Two officers in Williams Lake were forced to draw their side arms on two Natives from outside the area, one of whom reached into his pocket as the officers ordered them to stop. He dropped a loaded 9mm handgun. A search of them and their vehicle found another handgun, an AK-47 with forty live rounds, a .223 rifle, a zip gun, a stainless-steel tomahawk, lead pipe, pepper spray, nunchucks, three knives and a number of other weapons. These were hardly traditional fishing tools.

In the following days the same two men were involved in the armed standoff at Gustafson Lake near Williams Lake. It was a grim reminder to all our officers of the potential dangers they can face.

Officers even travelled from the East Coast to Lillooet to assist in patrols and I was patrolling with one of them one night in the Boston Bar area. Many of the trails are very steep and narrow and we were quietly walking down a trail when I slipped, carrying a $10,000 night scope. I found myself dangling from my elbows as loose rocks tumbled down the dark cliffs to the Fraser River below me and, remarkably, the scope was still in my hand.

I asked the other officer to slowly take the scope from my hand and then pull me back on the trail. We moved slowly and deliberately until we were both standing safely on the trail, gazing down into the darkness below. If I'd had time, I'm sure I would have crapped myself.

The summer patrol work and the improved relationships with First Nations made the salmon the obvious winners. Funding would be maintained for a while, but the usual chipping away at dollars started afterwards—until the next inquiry came along.

The Birthday Party

T he Lillooet bands' nighttime fishing closure greatly reduced the amount of illegal sales in the area but there were still a few long-time fish sellers willing to take a chance. Undercover fishery officers arranged a sale with one of the more infamous sellers near Merritt. The sale was to occur at the seller's residence in mid-afternoon.

We had several vehicles in the area watching when the undercover officers approached the house. The sale went without a hitch and the undercover officers gave the pre-arranged signal to come in and make the arrest. We pulled into the yard to a very upset fish seller. A number of young people came out of the house to see what was happening. It turned out the seller's twelve-year-old boy was holding a birthday party and I could tell we weren't invited.

We dealt with matters as quickly as possible and talked to a few of the kids. We knew they'd be told about the mean guys in green after we left so we wanted to talk to them ourselves. I pulled out a handful of DFO pins that I often carried and handed them out to the kids. The fish seller glared at me in anger. I just smiled and apologized to the kids for disrupting their birthday party. We seized 120 sockeye, gave the seller some paper and let the party carry on.

The next week we learned that Mr. Seller had continued his business but wasn't storing his fish at home any longer. He was hiding them in the most unlikely of places—in the walk-in freezer at a DFO hatchery. That was a twist!

Officers went to the chinook hatchery and seized the frozen sockeye. The storage of sockeye in a chinook hatchery was a very serious matter. The risk of disease transfer between sockeye and chinook is high and DFO policy aims to prevent any facility from having the two present at the same time.

The hatchery manager happened to be a friend of Mr. Seller and was allowing him to store the fish there. The contract for the hatchery manager was not renewed that fall. I later learned Mr. Seller's actions may have negated his chances at some provincial government contracts as well.

Both the men were very upset with me and responded the way some desperate people often do, claiming harassment and discrimination. Their actions had caused them to lose hundreds of thousands of dollars in government contracts, not to mention the cost of appearances in court.

It took a number of years but Mr. Seller and I were at last able to put aside our differences. I relied on him to help out in a number of potential conflicts around the region and he played a pivotal role in at least two protests that could not have been resolved without his help. I'll always be thankful for his efforts.

Canadian National Railway Problems

We were receiving reports of train crews buying fish from First Nations and taking them on the trains in coolers. The reports indicated that large amounts of salmon could be travelling right across the country.

We obtained a search warrant for a couple of Canadian National Railway engineers in Kamloops based on information received. The warrant was successful: we found both frozen and canned sockeye in two residences. The fish were seized, and the engineers charged.

We tried to watch the train crews in Boston Bar but the community is so small it was difficult to keep track without drawing suspicion. I decided to try a more open approach and arranged a meeting with a highly placed company officer in Vancouver. I also wanted to discuss the issue of train crews clearing the tracks of gravel and debris and throwing it into the river. The local crews hadn't co-operated with our efforts to stop the practice and I needed to get their attention.

I arrived at the executive's office and was taken to meet him. He was a very arrogant man and certainly didn't want to spend much time with me. I was taken aback by his derogatory comments about the train crews. He complained about how much they got paid and said other things that shouldn't be printed. I proceeded to tell him about the engineers we'd caught. I also said if we caught a crew with fish on the train, we would seize the train. He burst out laughing, "You can't do that! A stopped train would cost us $5,000 an hour."

I suggested we could and would seize a train, and I produced a copy of the *Fisheries Act* showing him the powers under which we'd do it. He was still laughing. He pointed out that the head of the railway company was a personal friend of the prime minister. I despise political threats. I asked him to call a lawyer and describe the events to him. I said I would wait outside his office until after the call but he asked me to stay and he placed a call.

The executive described the situation to the lawyer and asked if fishery officers had the power to seize trains. I didn't hear the lawyer's answer but I saw the smile leave his face. There were a few more questions before the he hung up the phone and said, "What can I do to help resolve this?" Even corporate arrogance and political connections have their limitations.

The now co-operative CNR officer and I developed a letter that was sent out to all train crews. The letter clearly stated that employees would immediately be fired if they were caught with illegal salmon on the trains. We agreed to address a second issue through site visits.

I returned to Kamloops and followed up with railway inspections. The crews were still not happy with us but relented and took us on a tour of the tracks. Material was piled in many locations along the track, some slumping over the bank into the river. Charging them would take months and it would be difficult to prove damage to fish so I tried the media approach.

I appeared in a TV interview talking about problems with material falling into the river. I talked about the material piled on the bank and suggested that it could cause a roadbed collapse and be a risk to train crews. I had just hit a home run.

The next day the railway company was busy clearing the

material from the banks. It turns out my reference to the material being unsafe was accurate and the company was desperately trying to avoid a mishap. The train union president called me at home and thanked me for raising the issue. Train crews and railway management had become born-again environmentalists overnight and worked with us over the following months to resolve the situation.

Media to the Rescue

The fish managers decided to close the Fraser River to First Nations fishers in 1999 due to conservation concerns for sockeye. The managers have the difficult task of guessing how many fish will return based on spawning escapements from four years earlier and the number of smolts that left the river.

The problem is there are so many variables impacting the runs before they return to the coast. Estimating salmon returns is much like forecasting the weather: when the forecast is right no one remembers and when it's wrong no one forgets. Increased climate change, habitat loss, legal fisheries, poaching, water flows and a host of other factors all contribute to reduced returns. Perhaps it's time to forgo any estimation for salmon returns until they reach the coast; at least that way the fishery would be based on more realistic numbers.

Regardless of when the decisions are made for run estimation, the task of closing the river when earlier estimates prove to have been too high always rests on the fishery officers. The fishery officers have had to deal with far too many irate First Nations when "snap" closures are announced.

The DFO staff all know conservation comes first but far too

many managers get pressured to open fisheries before the numbers of fish are high enough. Of course the fishing of stocks in approach waters only exacerbates the low return issue and infuriates those who planned on fishing in the river.

Back to Lillooet in 1999, where such an announcement had made the local bands very upset and they had vowed to ignore the closure and fish. It's not that they didn't agree with conservation; they were just fed up with the commercial and sport fishers having already fished the stocks they were expected to leave alone.

On August 12, I was directed to get all the officers I needed to enforce the closure the following day. I dreaded the thought because I had vivid recollections of a number of serious protests in the past. I went home and considered my options.

After a series of phone calls I contacted the director, Terry Tebb, in Vancouver and arranged for him to meet with the chiefs and me the next day. Talking is always a good start to avoid a confrontation. I was torn about calling in officers and made the very difficult decision not to call any until we had at least met with the chiefs. I struggled with the decision because I had been directed to do it. It was a long, sleepless night.

The following morning Stu Cartwright and I travelled to Lillooet to meet with the director and the chiefs to discuss the issues. The meeting was brief and unsuccessful in averting the two hundred protesters from fishing. They were angry and told us they would not meet with us again. I still didn't want to call in twenty or thirty officers to face an angry group of two hundred but my choices were few.

I then made the unusual move of contacting the media about the event. I had established a trusting relationship with several media outlets in Kamloops and felt their involvement could help resolve the conflict. Most managers would never give the go-ahead to what I did because they don't take the time to work with the media.

The media will usually run or print a story based on the information they receive but too often government employees need approval from Ottawa (under any government) to contact the media and the process can take days or even weeks. I chose to work with and educate the media and build their trust.

I called Susan Edgell of TV7 in Kamloops to suggest they do a balanced story involving input from both sides (DFO and First Nations). I thought they would get a newsworthy story but if they chose to do a one-sided confrontational story the conflict could develop into a national incident. Susan offered to do a balanced story, probably because we trusted each other and understood the consequences.

I asked the reporters to travel to Lillooet and meet with the chiefs before we did to assure them their story would be heard. I arrived in Lillooet and met with Susan later in the day to be interviewed. After my interview she commented on how similar the issues and concerns were with both DFO and the First Nations. We had both emphasized the need for conservation and had talked about other fisheries having been opened and the need for fish in the community. Her comments didn't surprise me but they did give me an idea.

I asked the media crew to return to the river where the chiefs and two hundred protesters were gathered and show them the interview I had just given. Again, this was an unusual request that could only happen if people trust each other. The reporter did as I requested and the chiefs saw and heard my entire interview.

I was still pondering my next move when the media returned from the river. The chiefs were moved by the words I'd spoken to the media and had decided they would meet with us. The three of us—Stu, the director and myself—were invited to the Bridge River Rapids at 10 p.m. that day. Mixed emotions raced through us as we considered the risk of walking down a trail in the dark to a very large group of angry people.

We did take the walk. I never told the director my thoughts but I knew I could run faster than him and I think Stu could too. The evening was very dark and a torrential downpour had us soaked before we reached the bonfire by the river. No problem; we couldn't get any wetter!

About sixty people, including the chiefs, were gathered around a fire. The director was asked to speak first. He'd only spoken for a few minutes before he was interrupted and told he was done. His words about the need for a closure didn't go over well. We stood and listened as the chiefs stepped forward one by one and spoke to all the people around us. Each of them took a pinch of tobacco from a pouch and threw it into the fire before speaking. Their message was clear and they would all be fishing the next day. Whenever someone in the crowd agreed with a comment from a chief they would utter an owl-like hoot, nothing I'd heard before but obviously a traditional way to show support while someone was speaking.

A man holding a rattle emerged from the crowd and started dancing. There were no words, just dancing to the rattle and some drums in the crowd. His gaze was distant and he moved as if in a trance. I later learned he had performed a war dance. I was glad I hadn't seen it before.

The dancer stopped, almost collapsing from exhaustion, and someone helped him move from the fire before other chiefs stepped forward and continued. The last chief was closing the gathering when I decided I had to try something. I stepped forward and asked for permission to speak. After several glances among the chiefs I was permitted to come to the fire. I reached into the pouch and threw some tobacco into the fire. I didn't know the meaning of the action at the time but I wanted to follow their tradition and hoped I wasn't making a mistake. (I later learned the pinch of tobacco in the fire is a gesture to the Creator in the hopes things will be better in the future.)

I had no idea what I'd say when I stepped forward, but I spoke from the heart. I thanked them for letting me step near the fire because I was cold. A few laughed and others stared and waited. It was probably good I was wet from the rain because I think I'd have been wet from sweat. I talked about my first trip to Lillooet when I was twenty years old, when I had waited in the hills in case I'd be called into the violent protest unfolding by the river. I told them

I was scared then and was scared again today. I told them I had a family and believed most of them did too. I wanted to know why we couldn't resolve this without violence and without risk to our families.

I also told them I'd been directed to bring in teams of fishery officers and arrest those fishing. I told them I hadn't followed those directions because I wanted to try resolving this in a new way. I heard a few hoots of agreement and carried on with some confidence. I thanked them and stepped back. More hoots were echoed as I stepped back.

The chiefs gathered in a tight circle before the leader spoke. He thanked me for speaking from the heart. They agreed to meet the next day and agreed they would not be fishing until after we met. I approached the chiefs and shook their hands. All they wanted was a licence for a few elders to catch some fish. It was evident my words connected. It was a monumental occasion that few in DFO have ever heard about. Only bad news seems to travel fast in government.

The next morning it was agreed to have a few elders fish to a maximum of a hundred fish. This was a small price to pay for their co-operation for a closure for which they were not responsible. In the end they only caught about twenty-five fish but that wasn't the point. It was more about the respect shown on the river, respect that has carried on for many years.

There are still those who fish or sell fish illegally but the general relationship between DFO and First Nations in Lillooet has continued to grow in a positive way. Every year brings new challenges and the positive spirit could end in a flash unless more long-term solutions are developed. No doubt some reading this will disagree, but every confrontation or battle in history has ended with some form of negotiation or agreement. Why not forgo the battle and just work it out?

I've often thought about that cold, wet night on the river and what could have happened. In hindsight, if I had made that call to bring in fishery officers, it could have been the largest First

Nations protest in history and would probably have resulted in injuries or worse. Full credit must go to the reporter, Susan Edgell and TV7 in Kamloops, to Stu Cartwright, Terry Tebb and all the chiefs who found it in themselves to move past our dark history and were willing to work together. I hope this co-operation continues until governments finally make real attempts to settle First Nations issues.

Those who don't see resolving First Nations issues as a priority should learn more about history and the constitution. Those that do agree should elect a government that takes treaty rights seriously.

Running Scared

The worst part about being a manager was not chasing poachers. I felt like a border collie without cattle to chase. I still ran a lot in 2000, entering twenty-two races that year and winning my age group in all but one. There are always a few funny stories to tell when you spend that much time on the road.

I was leading a half-marathon race in Kamloops early one Sunday morning. The course looped through Kamloops, crossing the Kamloops Indian Reserve after eight miles. The serenity of the sunny morning was shattered by a chomping, growling pit bull running at my heels. I found another gear and sprinted away unharmed. I looked back as other runners ran past it but the dog didn't chase them. I wondered if the dog from the reserve knew I worked for DFO or whether perhaps his owner had recognized me.

On another morning I had taken my daughter to Shumway Lake for her rowing practice. I had a couple of hours to spare and decided to go for a run. I didn't run on the road but instead headed up the steep grassy slopes near the lake. It was a hot, sunny day and I kept climbing the hills, crossing the occasional barbed-wire fence. I came over a knoll after about six miles and noticed a pickup parked by a corral and two men working inside.

Two cowboys high on a cattle squeeze in the middle of the corral didn't know I was watching the entertainment as a young bull ran around the cattle squeeze, keeping the men from getting to the fence. The bull had a large growth on his eye and the men had sprayed something on it to stop the infection. The bull was now on the rampage, snorting and pawing dirt.

I could hear the two cowboys talking about their dilemma: if only one of them could get to the fence and open the gate without getting rammed by the bull. One tried to climb down only to be chased back as the bull rounded the squeeze. I watched for several minutes and then yelled out, "Do you need a hand? I can open the gate." One cowboy nearly fell off the fence when he heard my voice. They told me to leave because the bull was dangerous.

I stood a few more minutes before one of the cowboys relented and asked if I could open the gate. The bull ran out, leaving the two bewildered cowboys looking at me wearing running shorts and a singlet. "Where did you come from?" one asked. "Oh, I ran up from Shumway Lake." That didn't seem to explain anything to him; he said, "But that's six miles downhill that way. How did you get here?" I told him again that I had run. They just shook their heads and thanked me before I took off down the hill and back to the lake.

Restorative Justice

Jim Michie was a fishery officer in Williams Lake who invited me to attend a First Nations healing circle after a serious criminal case in the area. Like most enforcement officers, I had not witnessed such an event but had my own naive, biased view on its effectiveness in enforcement. I felt restorative justice (RJ) might serve a purpose in some minor cases but not for serious fishing matters. I was about to learn otherwise.

Jim had taken the very progressive step of working with the First Nations to develop an enforcement protocol between the RCMP, DFO, the Conservation Officer Service and the band. RJ can only work if the band and the accused are willing to follow through. If either isn't supportive of the initiative, the courts should be used.

I travelled to the reserve near Williams Lake to witness the healing circle for a woman who'd been abused by her husband. The woman, her sixteen-year-old son and the accused all had to speak before the group of local elders and government officials. The experience gave me a first hand look at RJ and changed my opinions entirely. The process dealt with the incident quickly whereas the courts could have taken months or even years. RJ gave all involved a chance to express how they felt; the courts rarely provide this opportunity, although that is changing as well.

I talked to Jim about RJ and agreed to support him working with Charlene Belleau on some DFO cases. The results were instant improvements in compliance, reduced recidivism (repeat offenders) and improved relationships between officers and the bands. Jim later became a regional champion providing training to all the officers in BC and the Yukon.

Not every case was successful and there are those who still don't agree with it but RJ has been successfully used in commercial fishing, recreation fishing and even a few habitat cases. I believe the successes will come as long as the support is given and it doesn't become bogged down with extensive policy that limits flexibility.

Brown-Nosers and Bobble-Heads

M any organizations are constricted by bobble-heads and brown-nosers. Brown-nosers are self-explanatory: those willing to stoop to any level if they think it might impress their boss, regardless of consequences to others. Brown-nosers can be found throughout an organization but can easily be spotted at meetings, and especially after meetings, desperately trying to impress the boss. Bobble-heads are those who sit in a meeting listening to one in charge speak and nod their head at every opportunity. The nod is meant to be a signal to the boss meaning I don't care what you say, or I'm with you and want to climb the corporate ladder, or I'm still awake. If the bobble-heads stop bobbing, a simple touch on the chin starts them again.

I was called one day and asked to apply to be the regional director of conservation and protection (C&P). I'd declined the invitation before but agreed to apply this time. I went through the lengthy application processes including the three-person interview panel. I didn't make the grade the first time and, curious to see where I could improve, I requested an interview with the man in charge. His responses were vague at first, but my questions became more pointed and the boss became more uncomfortable. Turns out, I had passed every question except one that I had only fallen one point short on. I finally said, "Look I've been around long enough to know that one point on one question would be adjusted if the board wanted me to pass, so what can I do to improve?" The boss squirmed and paused before saying, "Well Randy, the board just wasn't sure you'd do what you were told."

I said, "Thank you for being honest and thank you for making the right choice." He raised his eyebrows and I continued, "I'm not a bobble-head and if that's what you want, you've made the right decision. If you ever change your mind and want someone who will question the status quo and offer new ideas, give me a call, but thank you for not wasting our time." I left feeling good about the interview and waited for the right opportunity—and boss.

I know that good leaders are easy to follow but hard to find. I look back at all the people I worked for and those that worked for me. Too many people think they are a leader because they are in charge. They seldom take the time to talk to the staff holding the organization up and are the most dangerous.

I met many bobble-heads and brown-nosers in organizations, including in the RCMP, other federal agencies and the private sector. Fortunately there are enough good people willing to challenge the two and keep organizations working although the challenges become even greater in more senior positions. An opportunity arose in 2004 when a new boss asked me to apply for the same job I'd applied for six months earlier; this time I was successful.

The Williams Review

Sockeye returns to the Fraser River in 2004 were dismal and raised many unanswered questions. Public outcry demanded DFO hold another review just a short ten years after the last one (Fraser). Judge Brian Williams chaired the review along with ten panel members representing various stakeholder groups.

I was asked to prepare a forty-five-minute presentation on enforcement issues. The panel prepared a list of twenty-five questions for me to answer. Senior managers had not named me to testify; the panel had requested it. Although no one came out and said it directly, I knew some managers were concerned about my testimony. The only reason they would be concerned was that they knew I had told them about the issues year after year and they hadn't taken the necessary actions to address them. The increased enforcement funding resulting from the last review had slowly been chipped away and positions cut back to fund other shortfalls in the department.

I had five other officers seated with me during the presentation in case there were questions they could answer better than I. It was a bit risky, but I started my presentation with my daughter's hundred-word essay on the missing salmon from 1994:

The man in the picture is a biologist. He is holding a radio tag that was inserted into a live salmon this summer. The radio tag transmitted information such as location, water temperature, and the amount of fat left in the fish. Later this summer the water temperature was warmer than ever. This caused the fish to get confused and start swimming back downstream. The fish were low on energy and died. 1.3 million fish are missing from the river and never showed up to spawn. Some people think that it was from warm water temperatures and some think it is from poachers but like the tooth fairy nobody knows for sure.

—Dana Nelson, 11 years old

The panel members laughed and Judge Williams said, "She's got it figured out. Why are we here?" I continued with the forty-five-minute presentation that turned into one and a half hours with all the panel questions. At the conclusion the panel said they'd heard three weeks of testimony from DFO staff, and mine was the first where they felt they were getting straight answers. The comment didn't surprise me because I'd sat in on a few fish management staff presentations. I'll never understand why or how people can avoid telling the whole truth under oath.

One of the main goals of the presentation was to finally establish an enforcement branch within DFO. The recommendation had appeared in every review and inquiry for over thirty-five years; I'd listed at least ten of them in the presentation. The main downside of such a move to fish managers and directors would be a loss of their control over enforcement staff. Fishery officers and every report on the topic saw it as necessary and positive.

I ended with, "I am proud to be a fishery officer. I used to be proud of the department I represent. I want to help restore that pride. I would be willing to assist in delivery of the recommendations that may be forthcoming."

I noticed a senior fish manager seated in the room and I knew he'd been sent to take notes from my testimony. No manager had even bothered to ask me what I intended to say; I would have given anyone my presentation if they'd asked. He appeared nervous as I sat down beside him. I told him I'd give a copy of my presentation to whoever wanted it. No one should be surprised by the facts in it because they'd been presented many times before.

In the weeks after my testimony I learned that some people were attempting to discredit my testimony. I knew I had the facts to support everything I'd testified to and wasn't concerned. It was yet another reminder of how low some people will crawl. Some managers don't want to be bothered by facts, logic and common sense. Judge Williams and the panel were too knowledgeable about DFO to be distracted, and they made the right decisions.

In the end Judge Williams' report recommended an enforcement branch once again, along with many similar recommendations keying in on enforcement funding. The usual temporary funding came to fishery officers and the job was getting done.

Senior managers across the country banded together and attempted to stop the change to an enforcement branch. In the end the deputy minister supported a one-year pilot project for a regional enforcement manager reporting directly to the regional director general. This was a major victory and the right decision. However, it was a pilot. Pilots have a habit of continuing only until the heat is off and then things slowly revert to the way they were; I'd seen this movie many times over.

I was called to a meeting with the regional director general a week after the report's release. I believed in his leadership but was uncertain how he felt. He told me he'd heard I gave a passionate, factual presentation and his main concern was that I'd lost trust in the department. He wanted me to help out and act as the new regional director of enforcement. I gladly accepted when I learned of the structural change in the department that would mean all fishery officers would report to a person with enforcement experience (a recommendation that had been made many times by many inquiries over the preceding thirty-five years).

The one-year pilot went as I expected. Success stories were happening around the region with fishery officers; compliance was breaking out everywhere. I emphasized the need to work with other programs and build relationships with all users, especially First Nations. The pilot was so successful it was implemented permanently and later nationwide. Hopefully it'll never go back.

The changes didn't happen without some strong opposition from area directors though. They were concerned about losing control of conservation and protection (C&P) funding that had traditionally been used to shore up shortfalls in other programs. The new format finally gave enforcement control of its own resources.

The clearest example came at a meeting in Ottawa that I attended. The change in reporting structure meant I would attend the national fish management meetings with the very people that were unhappy with the change. This meeting was the first I'd attended. I had a conference call and missed an hour of the second morning but as I walked into the room everyone stopped talking and all eyes turned to me. I later learned they'd been talking about not wanting me in attendance, their main reason being that my counterparts in other regions didn't want me there.

I knew that to be false but I left the room and called each of my counterparts directly and asked them. Every one of them strongly supported my attendance.

I returned to the meeting armed with the truthful facts and asked for a moment to speak. I told the group I had just called every one of their C&P directors and they all supported my attendance. None of the managers at the meeting would look at me. They'd each told a big fat lie, except the one from Pacific Region, who'd supported my attendance. It was just another reminder of the deep-rooted resistance displayed by a group of selfish bureaucrats.

The regional approach to enforcement allowed the program to focus on regional priorities, move staff around without interference, work with the user groups and sit on the Regional Management Committee (RMC). Discussions at the RMC now included someone with extensive enforcement experience, rarely present in the past.

One of the most important results of the change was the reduced number of confrontations with First Nations. Decisions in the past had been made with little or no input from fishery officers and yet officers had had to enforce the decisions. Now officers had input before the decisions were made and could take time to interact more with the First Nations communities. Confrontations had not occurred in the six years after front-line reporting of fishery officers and I credit the change as a direct reason for the improvements to safety.

A Proud Day

O ur daughter Janna had graduated from university with a degree in Environmental Biology. She came home one day to tell us she'd applied to be a fishery officer. We had no idea she was

With Paul Steele, director general of conservation and protection, I proudly presented a badge to my daughter Janna as she graduated from fishery officer training.

interested and fully supported her, albeit with some apprehension. The dangers of the job came to my mind first.

DFO often gets over a thousand applicants for eight or ten positions and most new officers have related job experience. I knew the optics if she made it so I told the selection committee I didn't want to know any results until the final list was established.

Janna came through and made the cut. She was even picked as troop leader for the first half of her training. I was able to present her badge at the graduation. My brass buttons had to be sewn back on the next day. I told her she shouldn't feel any pressure to remain an officer if something else appealed to her.

Her first three years were spent in New Aiyansh, where she had lived for her first nine months of life twenty-five years earlier. I had many calls with her discussing some of the "characters" I'd dealt with when I worked in the area. I was amazed how many still had the same old habits.

Improving Morale

I wasn't sure what I would do as regional director of conservation and protection at first but I knew I wanted to improve staff morale. We'd made a number of changes that started improving things but, to quote my former boss John Hipp, morale was "lower than a snake's belly in a wagon rut."

The federal government conducted an employee survey every two years. That survey rated all fifty-five federal agencies in a number of areas including employee engagement. DFO's was low but when I took the fishery officers' responses out, we were lower than any other federal agency. We had nowhere to go but up.

I was scanning through the hundreds of emails I received each day and came across a resumé for a young employee working in Ottawa and noticed he wanted to move to BC. From his resumé he sounded like someone who could help so I called him up. Within days he was on his way to Vancouver. That was one of the best decisions I made as the director. Etienne Laliberté had helped develop the new hiring rules imposed on government and we had many problems with our staffing vacancies; Etienne might be the answer.

Etienne and I developed a special working friendship and shared many values such as taking care of people and providing openness to all staff. Despite criticism from our human resources (HR) branch for hiring him, I soon found that others wanted to hire him because we were improving so fast. We had our staffing process down to three weeks and filled the backlog of sixty-five percent of our supervisory positions. People want job security; acting doesn't fit the bill. Our open processes brought criticism from many "old school" HR workers but we kept moving. Staff learned they could trust the processes and appeals dropped dramatically.

We had staff help develop solutions to problems through workshops and meetings. Progress was slow and painful at first but quickly became the envy of other programs. We surveyed staff regularly. I held regional phone calls regularly to update staff on anything they might be interested in. Our grievance numbers dropped to near zero from hundreds per year.

We developed a training week for staff, held every two years. It gave staff opportunities to learn and to meet friends they were rarely able to see. The mood rocketed so fast we were concerned it could come crashing down just as quickly. Not everyone bought in and a few were left by the wayside. We invited twenty retired officers to our training session to deliver some training and interact with all the staff. They were delighted to attend and were inspiring for new staff to meet.

We held a formal dinner complete with awards and recognition for staff achievements. We even had Lieutenant-Governor Steven Point attend to hand out the exemplary service medals. We allowed staff to bring their families (at their cost) to the meeting.

I invited staff to identify problems but any problem they raised had to come with a list of potential solutions. My goal was "to communicate until I heard an echo." This meant talking to each other and listening until the message sounded the same from both sides. Often one side had to move, sometimes both, but in the end everyone was on the same page. I feel too many managers just speak and call it communication. Clearly it's not effective until everyone understands and moves forward. Supervisors were given a letter spelling out the expectations by which they'd be measured.

We took on the non-performers. I think they are the most time-consuming, challenging things a manager can face. Some respond and get their careers on track; others may choose to challenge and never change. Most employees appreciate managers dealing with the "anchors" that hold us back, resulting in improvements for everyone in the end. Too few supervisors deal with problem employees effectively; they choose to pass them on to someone else or ignore them. A poor employee can only result from a poor manager. I once sent a message to my supervisor when I was dealing with a poor performer. I stated, "I feel like I'm in a marathon. I don't fear the competition; I feel sorry for them."

I engaged the union in the early stages of any issue I thought needed attention. I developed a trust relationship with the union, bewildering many other managers. Many managers actually suggested it was dangerous to share such information with the union. I saw only positive results when I did. I encouraged staff to use fewer emails and my own email traffic dropped from between 150 and 200 a day to 40 or 50. I encouraged staff to actually talk to people rather than email.

I sent a birthday card to each of the two hundred staff on their birthday. I hand-wrote a note and signed each one of them. It was amazing to hear how appreciative such a gesture can be. I wanted people to have some fun and it was becoming contagious.

The employee survey three years later moved the fishery officer result from dead last to number two of fifty-five departments. It happened as the result of some new ideas driven from the ground up, of Etienne leading the staffing, of informing staff regularly and working with the union.

Some other managers wanted to know our secret. They were surprised to hear that most of the steps, although very time-consuming, were simple, but some managers remained skeptical and never changed. They'd rather blame their staff for not listening. Successful managers don't have to have a bunch of letters or degrees after their name; the most important asset is a degree in common sense.

Etienne Laliberté was one of the brightest people I've ever worked with. His only downfall was speaking the truth to power, a trait I admire. After a long and disgusting series of incidents of mistreatment and harassment by senior management, he left the department. I was extremely disappointed with the vile, underhanded actions of some people in handling his situation.

In the middle of our success I was told my acting assignment might end. The entry in my diary that evening read, "I sure have enjoyed the ride and I will find a pony in this pile of horse shit!" The pony arrived when I won the competition and was appointed to the job permanently.

I had many weeks of eighty to ninety hours' work but I enjoyed it. I knew it wouldn't be forever. I also knew it wasn't healthy to work that much. I had some crazy dreams and wrote about one in my diary: I was halibut fishing on a lake in Saskatchewan with another officer but didn't have any luck. Another officer came in with a large halibut and let me borrow the secret lure. It was a large plug with purple rhinestones and sequins of all colours on it. I hooked a fish from the dock and jumped into a small boat to land it. The fish got hung up in a barbed-wire fence and I landed it by roping it on the tail. After that dream I knew I had become a senior manager! I also shared the dream with all the staff on my next conference call. You have to make fun of yourself sometimes.

The Cohen Commission

T he Cohen Commission on Fraser River sockeye was
announced in 2010. The public was hungry for answers
about what was affecting the iconic Fraser River sockeye. A
public outcry against aquaculture threatened to focus too much
attention on this as a cause while internally it seemed DFO wanted
to focus on science and the unknown ocean survival of salmon.
Enforcement received little attention until the public and the
commission included it as a key item to review.

I know some managers became nervous about conservation
and protection (C&P) testifying, given the history of previous
inquiries always pointing to the scaling back of enforcement. Even
though every review in history criticized DFO for reducing funding
and officers, DFO was once again facing this glaring issue only
five years after the Williams Review. Ottawa and senior managers
scrambled to portray a picture of increased funding but even the
best statistical chefs could not cook this one.

A C&P management team of thirteen staff with 350 years of
experience met for a week to prepare the real unabashed financial
numbers for the commission. Senior DFO finally had a taste of
what field staff face, although from a very different angle. Ottawa

couldn't control the agenda nor answer the questions for C&P. The truth would be revealed and many were squirming.

I knew I was under a microscope and never felt a shred of support from above while preparing the material for Justice Cohen. I also wanted to ensure no one could claim they didn't know the facts. I met with every level of the organization up to and including the deputy minister to inform them of my intended message. The information had been provided many times before and ignored. I even tried to meet with the minister's adviser only to receive a directive from upstairs three hours later informing me that no one could meet with the minister's adviser without regional approval. Things were getting testy. Why wouldn't they want the minister's office to know the facts? Obviously they had delivered a different message from the one that I had and feared the truth once again.

The more I informed the department of my concerns, the more alienated I felt. I reviewed a six-foot-high stack of binders and documents provided by other lawyers interested in asking enforcement questions. At one point I met with a non-DFO person, familiar with both inquiries and DFO, with whom I'd developed a trusting relationship. I wanted to talk to a senior person who understood the process and that I knew I could trust. It's sad that he had to be from outside of DFO. I met with retired judge Barry Stuart and discussed the problems I faced. He told me, "You are who you say you are. I've never met anyone who's been in government as long as you and has maintained his values." His encouraging words helped me move on.

This was going to be lonely but I knew the organization needed a little surgery, not a bandage. I was constantly reminded of many experiences while working in the field over my career and not being supported. An organization cannot be healthy unless the foundation is solid. The support of field staff was a strong motivator.

The inspiration of the late Bill Otway (outspoken critic, former DFO employee and long-time leader with the BC Wildlife Fedration) also compelled a push forward. I and three other senior C&P staff had met with Bill during the late stages of his battle with cancer. Even though Bill was near death he still urged us to tell the story and keep up the fight for the fish because no one else would. He died seven days later.

After I testified someone in Ottawa was tasked with reviewing every word of my testimony to try and find inaccuracies. I told him if he found anything at all to call me immediately; he never called.

The commissioner had asked for ideas or recommendations when I first testified, and I prepared a list of thirty-two ideas to provide him when I testified the second time. There was no support for presenting them. I told a few people I was the one under oath and I would tell the truth and answer any question I was asked.

When I testified the second time I provided the commissioner with the recommendations and he thanked me. Neither DFO nor their lawyers were happy but many of the recommendations were included in Justice Cohen's final report.

At one point in my testimony I compared the workload of fishery officers between regions. I compared the Pacific Region to Maritime regions and found the following facts:

- Pacific Region handles half of all the violations in Canada with one-third of the officers.
- There are 600 First Nations bands in Canada; 200 are in Pacific Region.
- Pacific Region has about 400,000 recreational fishers on the oceans and the largest salmon freshwater fishery in North America, far greater than all eastern regions combined.
- The landed value of fish in Pacific Region is greater than any of the eastern regions (DFO 2010 documents).
- Habitat work is greater than in any eastern region.
- Pacific has the largest number of listed species under the *Species at Risk Act*.
- Pacific has 27,000 miles of coastline, more than most eastern regions and the same as Newfoundland.
- The land area of Pacific Region is 14.3 percent of the country; the four Maritimes combined are 5.8 percent.

British Columbians expect to catch salmon off our coast. They also expect DFO to protect this precious resource through properly funded enforcement programs.

- The miles of salmon streams are greater than those in all the Maritimes combined.
- The ratio of fishery officers to residents is 1:24,000 in the Pacific Region, 1:4,600 in Newfoundland, 1:8,000 in Gulf Region and 1:6,000in Maritimes Region.

I also discovered that the Pacific Region has a higher number of resource managers compared to fishery officers than any other region. Internally staff argued that it's because of the complexity of fisheries and the number of stakeholders to deal with, and I agree with that, but the number of enforcement staff to deal with those same complexities should follow. The "West Against the Rest" mentality is alive and well in DFO.

Justice Cohen seemed very attentive during all the testimony and seemed especially interested in the enforcement story he heard. During my testimony he asked how I intended to deal with getting the job done in the face of all the reductions and workload.

My reply was "I plan to retire." I also testified a permanent solution be reached with $12 million to $14 million added to 2012 annual funding levels.

All three reviews and inquiries I participated in have remarkable similarities. DFO senior staff and Ottawa desperately tried to control the direction of the review and their staff. Then, when the report pointed out obvious problems they had known about for years, sometimes decades, they worked tirelessly to try spinning a response without dealing with the real issue. If that worked, they moved on. If it didn't manage the noise, they developed an interim approach that might include temporary funding and slowly scaling the funding back until the public forgot about them. Very few recommendations were dealt with permanently.

Sadly, the Pacific DFO region is quietly closing a number of field offices, with plans to relocate the staff to new patrol boats being built for the coast. It's important the new boats have officers aboard but resources should have been assigned to the boats, not stolen from inadequate numbers that already exist. Better still, why not train some Coast Guard staff in enforcement and have them work with all enforcement agencies? It makes no sense to have a Coast Guard service that has minimal, if any, enforcement powers.

None of Justice Cohen's recommendations had been implemented a year and a half after the report was released. Many recommendations referred to aquaculture; the only government response to date (January 2014) has been the lifting of a moratorium on new applications (contrary to recommendations). We could have shored up the sagging funding for many years if the millions of dollars spent on holding the inquiry had been directed to DFO budgets. I'm sure we'd see instant action if only salmon could cast votes.

Aquaculture

The BC coast is one of the best places in the world for aquaculture production. It's also one of the most productive areas in the world for wild salmon. Unfortunately the development of this industry took place with a "gold rush" mentality, with minimal regard for other users and existing resources.

Aquaculture is the only industry I'm aware of that is allowed to discharge raw, untreated effluent and chemicals into fish-bearing waters. We expect other industries, agriculture and cattle producers to keep chemicals and animal waste out of watercourses but aquaculture gets a free pass. The remoteness of salmon farms puts them out of sight, out of mind of the mainstream public, who remain unaware of harms the farms may be inflicting on the marine environment.

The industry's apparent lack of regard for other resources is shown in the following two glaring examples. The first involved the reported entanglement of a sea lion in the nets designed to keep sea mammals out of the net pens. It seems seals and sea lions like to feast upon the salmon contained within the pens. Fishery officers conducted an inspection of the net pen and located over fifty dead sea lions hanging like grapes from the netting below the ponds. The shocking discovery was never properly investigated, mainly due to inadequate resources to undertake a detailed investigation. How many other operations are having an impact on seals and sea lions? The number of officers hired to monitor aquaculture was less than half of what was requested to properly inspect and monitor the industry.

Another sad example involved an aquaculture industry representative who'd chartered a sport fishing trip on the West Coast. The guide provided the opportunity and the aquaculture rep was successfully angling and catching chinook salmon. At one point the guide netted another chinook, brought it aboard the boat and asked, "Do you want to keep this one?" The response was, "Of course. Any wild fish I can take will be less competition for aquaculture." It wasn't a joke.

The number of aquaculture operations and their remoteness makes it nearly impossible for fishery officers and habitat staff to properly monitor and assess the impacts of the industry. I don't blame those in DFO who promote aquaculture; they are probably doing what they've been told.

It would seem the industry could move to closed containment ponds for fish production and avoid any interaction with or impacts on wild fisheries resources. The industry might howl about the costs, however. I understand the average aquaculture site can cost $2.5 million to $3 million to build (by 2011 estimates) and will turn a profit in about two and a half years. What other investment can guarantee that type of return? The cost of closed containment would increase production costs but would certainly be affordable and vastly reduce potential impacts on wild marine resources.

Improving Relationships

Another positive development in the growth of conservation and protection (C&P) was the establishment of an RCMP liaison officer. An RCMP inspector was hired to work in DFO headquarters, providing a link to the RCMP. This vital position helped build trust and improve the understanding of both agencies.

The inspectors I worked with most were Cal Chrustie and Mike Carlson. Cal was especially skilled at conflict negotiations and worked tirelessly with our officers and First Nations groups. Cal's skills and honesty helped restore trust between all of us, including the RCMP and DFO.

Mike Carlson brought a wealth of knowledge from the RCMP as well and he worked equally hard to improve the administration of our enforcement group. Both men were so positive and professional and moved us light years ahead as an organization.

The field support fishery officers received from the RCMP happened because of the liaison positions. This was especially evident in the Chilliwack area where an RCMP officer, Chris Gosselin, worked tirelessly to assist C&P in the First Nations community dealing with serious criminals and helping build relationships with the community and their leadership.

Fishery officers have further improved relationships with First

Nations through hard work and training. New fishery officers are given some true cultural training that can include sweats and conversations with elders.

Fishery officers organize a First Nations Youth Conference where youth are selected by bands and sent along with an elder and local fishery officer for training and education that results in better understanding on all sides.

The improvement of relationships between fishery officers and First Nations is growing throughout BC and the Yukon. At the time of writing this book, there hasn't been a single serious confrontation in nearly seven years. It's taken a lot of hard work on both sides and must continue to grow. Clearly, purchasing large canoes and participating in shared journeys has been a growth opportunity that many fishery officers and First Nations have enjoyed. The first canoe was difficult to justify but has exceeded expectations through improved understanding, ultimately benefiting the fisheries resource.

In 2012, fishery officers purchased a second large canoe and invited me to the launch on the Okanagan Journey. A group of fifteen fishery officers stood around the tarp-covered canoe while First Nations paddlers in several canoes looked on from the water. When the tarp was pulled off I was speechless! The canoe was called the R.A. Nelson. After a few hard swallows I thanked them for their recognition. I also pointed out that DFO vessels were generally named in honour of individuals after they died but perhaps that didn't apply to canoes. We carried the canoe into the water and I dove under for a traditional cleansing before the cheering crowd.

I received a call from a fishery officer after I retired explaining that a First Nations artist wanted to paint the canoe. Several months later I attended a second unveiling of the canoe in Kamloops with about twenty DFO staff and First Nations representatives. The canoe was covered with traditional images from petroglyphs in the Shuswap territory. My name still appeared near the bow but the Shuswap words Cwiselc re Sk'elep (meaning Running Coyote, my new name in Shuswap) had also been inscribed by the artist,

Fishery officers surprised me by placing my name on a large canoe used in relationship building and cultural exchanges with First Nations and other enforcement agencies.

Roxane McCallum. Roxane proceeded to read a story she'd written about the journey of Running Coyote. Each of the images on the canoe represented part of my time with DFO. She spoke of the coyote being a trickster, able to run long distances, and she talked of the importance of family, trying to remain true to moral values, experiencing many hardships along the way but ultimately ending in a good place surrounded by First Nations friends and DFO friends. I was smiling inside—like a coyote from Hodgeville I guess.

In 2013 I paddled in the Kamloops area with over two hundred First Nations members, fishery officers and police officers. The irony was overwhelming: some twenty-five years earlier I had been in the middle of "Oar Wars" with a group of First Nations, swinging oars at each other, and now I was in a canoe pulling on paddles together with First Nations people and travelling in the same direction. The Shuswap bands participating in the journey had only recently acquired canoes and they thanked DFO for helping them renew a lost tradition. I know we would all benefit by taking bolder steps outside our comfort zones. Certainly the fish would be happier! Maybe some land claims discussions should occur in a canoe and not a boardroom!

Epilogue: Smiling Until the End

Some of you reading the last few chapters may be asking, "Where are the funny stories?" I apologize if you found them less entertaining than earlier stories, but I hope you found them enlightening.

My tenure as regional director of conservation and protection lasted until I retired after thirty-five years as a fishery officer. I challenged the status quo at times throughout my career but I still think DFO is one of the best organizations one could ever work for. DFO is the oldest enforcement agency in Canada, formed right after Confederation in 1867. The Canadian Navy's first vessels came from the DFO fleet. Fishery officers have a proud past that few in the general public are aware of.

The job of a fish or wildlife officer in North America is also extremely dangerous. North American statistics show that a fish or wildlife officer is eight times more likely to be killed on the job than a police officer. One reason for this could be that while BC has one police officer for every 500 residents, the total fish and wildlife agencies within BC serve the public with one officer for every 13,300 residents.

The remoteness of their work often results in fishery officers searching for drowning victims, performing emergency first aid and recovering bodies. DFO has the best small boats and trained officers to search many of our rivers and watercourses in BC, and we are frequently asked to lead searches for victims. One officer who worked on the lower Fraser River recovered over thirty drowning victims in his career. Fortunately, I've only been involved in a few such recoveries, but one of the drowning victims had been in the water for seven weeks. Enough said. The best way to cope with this difficult task was to focus on the appreciative families who were now able to find closure.

Officers receive special wilderness first-aid training and are often called upon to help people in distress. In one incident, fishery officers Mike Weston and Bryan Jubinville performed CPR on a commercial gillnet fishermen who'd experienced a heart attack while fishing with his sixteen-year-old son. The two officers administered CPR for over an hour while lifting the man into their boat and taking him to the nearest road to a waiting ambulance. Sadly the man perished but the family was extremely grateful for their efforts.

It's hard to describe why men and women choose this profession, given the lower wages and the higher risks, and yet annual recruitments of between eight and ten officers draw well over a thousand applicants. The standards are more rigorous than for any other entry process I'm aware of. Officers are certainly not all perfect but I have never heard of a validated complaint about the improper use of force or mistreatment of clients. Additionally, relationships with First Nations have improved dramatically through a lot of hard work on both sides. Take the time some day to thank them for what they do.

I had so much fun I almost felt guilty getting paid some days; others felt like a prison. I managed to retire with the same philosophy as when I hired on: have some fun, be honest above reproach, catch the bad guys (inside or outside the department), support the bottom as well as the top and then have some more fun. I walked out the door having made a lot of friends and a few enemies. I travelled the entire province and spent time in areas of the country that few have seen. The job took me to every province and territory except Nunavut.

I look back at things early in my career that caused me stress. In later years these same events wouldn't even change my pulse. I guess it's called getting older and wiser but I truly believe nothing in the world causes you stress: it's your reaction to things happening that builds stress. Find the right balance and most days can be fun.

The last thing I want to say is the most important and that is to thank Lorraine for being with me the whole ride. She not only put up with my long hours of work; I also ran over 60,000 miles and curled about 2,500 games over my career. She suffered many sleepless nights, phone calls at home, harassment from the public, and unpaid work. I couldn't find another person so understanding and supportive.

Thanks to you, too, for reading my story!